Thomas Donohue

Popular Progress

The Cause of Agricultural and Industrial Depression

Thomas Donohue

Popular Progress
The Cause of Agricultural and Industrial Depression

ISBN/EAN: 9783744694124

Printed in Europe, USA, Canada, Australia, Japan

Cover: Foto ©Andreas Hilbeck / pixelio.de

More available books at **www.hansebooks.com**

POPULAR PROGRESS

THE CAUSE OF AGRICULTURAL AND INDUSTRIAL DEPRESSION,

AND

THE REMEDY.

BY

Rev. THOMAS DONOHOE, D. D.

Author of "THE IROQUOS AND THE JESUITS"

BUFFALO, N. Y.:
PRESS OF MURRAY & DAWSON.
1898.

PREFACE.

Are the ebb and flow of our prosperity produced by accidental causes, or is there something radically wrong in the industrial system, which produces such general and long-continued depression in a country of such vast resources?

Every good citizen must grieve to behold desolation spreading through this fair land, in the wake of that insatiable monster, "hard times," that has been devouring the substance of the poor and has crushed out many a feeble life; and his heart must yearn for the day when prosperity shall again smile on the toiler's task and bring happiness and comfort to his home.

That there has been a great deal of suffering in the land is a lamentable fact, too often ignored by state and national authorities, because there has been no general clamor for relief; and as poverty in the eyes of society is a sin or a crime, people would prefer to suffer in silence rather than make known their weakness or guilt.

IV.

When a plague sweeps over the land, marking its path with suffering, with ruin and with death, the sympathy and the generosity of a noble people are aroused, and all the skill and intelligence that money can procure or that authority can compel are brought into play, to bring relief and restore health to the land. The industrial plague, known as "hard times," is more insidious in its nature, more mysterious in its origin than any physical epidemic; yet, it is no less far reaching in its effects and disastrous in its results. The physical plague will mark its victims with outward and unmistakable symptoms of disease, but the industrial malady merely marks the gaunt features of its prey with the lines of want and care, or clutches the heart, and stifles every outward evidence of shameful weakness.

The two great political parties have promised that the adoption of their principles would bring a panacea for all our ills, and would even restore healthful conditions to the land, but hope too long deferred has wearied and made sad the hearts of a patient people.

V.

If we can discover the true cause of our malady, it should be within our province to effect a cure.

The land yields immense food crops; so abundant, in fact, are these crops some years that it does not pay to harvest them, and they are allowed to rot in the fields, or our consuls and merchants seek a market in foreign countries for the surplus products that cannot be sold at home; and all this time strong, able-bodied men with willing hands, often skilled in special callings, are starving in sight of plenty. Our manufactures, mines, etc., like the land, turn out more products than can be consumed; yet, there are hundreds of thousands of idle hands, but they have no work and can get no money to buy the comforts, or even the necessaries of life.

This country should not only be the land of plenty, but also the home of peace. Isolated from the great powers of the world by immense tracts of ocean, and with a smaller neighbor pursuing kindred interests on her northern border, she need not fear any external enemy, and should not have any internal foe. People govern themselves, at least in theory, and make their own laws; and if prosperity can be controlled by government or law, then the remedy is within easy reach.

When men see plenty all about them, of which they are denied a part, and luxury in which they cannot share, though they may be able and willing to toil for a pittance, they cannot be in love with conditions which seem to cast all nature's favors at the feet of the few. These men may have families, may have little ones at home looking for the coming of the bread winner, "bearing his sheaves," and then want will breed discontent and incipient rebellion.

Shall the strong protect and help the weak; or is warfare the natural condition of man, and the brute struggle for the survival of the fittest the ultimate destiny of the race? As this is the age of reason, all disputes should be settled by appeal to the higher intelligence, and in no land should this be so easily effected as here where the governing power is in the hands of the people. Rumblings of discontent may be heard, but they are only the bellowings of brute force, manifest-

ing by dumb, but intelligible appeal, the revolt
of the great army of toilers against the injustice
of the present industrial system. Anarchy, too,
and socialism, favored by disturbed conditions,
like dark clouds, may be seen above the horizon
portending storms and destruction.

This country has passed through many great
crises in her history, but the good sense and
patriotism of her people have rallied to her
cause and have enabled her to triumph. The
proper province of Government is to promote the
welfare of its people, not indeed by providing
happiness, but by placing within the reach of all
the means of procuring happiness for themselves
by their exertion and toil. If conditions have
arisen which tend to limit the means of procuring a livelihood, and thus exclude a large portion
of citizens from the pursuits of happiness, it is
the duty of Government to re-adjust those conditions to the requirements of the public welfare.
This is not paternalism; it is justice.

The author has sought to point out the facts
and to suggest methods of relief; and if this
little work only serves to throw some light upon

the true causes of and the remedies for industrial depressions, his labors shall not have been in vain.

It is well that one free from the traditional theories and the meaningless cant of the schools, and independent of the crude aspirations and the aims of organized labor, should discuss questions which have such important bearing upon the prosperity and civilization of America.

THOMAS DONOHOE.

Buffalo, N. Y., February, 1898.

INDEX.

CHAPTER I.

AGRICULTURE.

Agriculture claimed the first attention of the human race. The fields yielded teeming harvests to the careful tillers of the soil; herds and flocks supplied food and raiment in abundance, whilst varied cares and rural scenes made life pleasant amid God's creation.

In every newly-settled land the first occupation of the settler is the tilling of the soil, for in this way may be found all that is needed to supply the wants of incipient society. The early American colonists cultivated a bit of cleared ground, whilst they built their rude log cabins for shelter and sought in the hunt the furs of wild animals to barter at the trading posts for the products of Europe.

Agriculture was the staple of work and the standard of wages. In the colonial period there was very little manufacture in the land. Women of the farm carded and spun the wool, and wove the cloth for the household, and bartered the surplus for luxuries or for the articles of urban or

foreign make. The wages* paid the farm hand
regulated the pay in every other branch of industry. Laborers were scarce,** and the supply
was not equal to the demand. Men preferred
the independence of individual ownership to sub-
servient employment, especially as the former
was an easy road to comparative affluence.

The advantages of farm life were not swept
aside by the advancing tide of immigration, but
continued and even increased up to the last
twenty-five or thirty years. The great number
of men prominent in every walk of life, who
were reared on the farm, prove plainly that this
calling is eminently suited to nourish all the
elements of independent, sturdy manhood. The
pleasant, prosperous homes that dotted the land
until recent years tell us clearly that men engaged in this field of industry attained wealth as
well as independence. Men will seek lucrative
employment or occupation, even though it en-

*Wages, for some years, was established by law.
In 1633 the Massachusetts Bay Colony decided that
two shillings without board, 'or fourteen pence
with board, a day, should be the pay of mechanics. (Carroll D. Wright).
**Hence, the introduction of slavery.

tails physical discomfort or the loss of social
amenity. As long as fields yielded remunerative
returns for the labor expended on them, men
were ready to till them, and any loss of social
comfort could be easily compensated by the
monetary reward of farm life. As soon as agriculture ceased to make a fair return for the capital and labor expended, it lost also its charm, and
people, especially the young, sought more lucrative and attractive opportunities in the towns.
Until twenty-five or thirty years ago the condition of the farm owner, or even the farm laborer,
was vastly superior to that of the laborer or
artisan of the town. The farm owner could pay
for his farm in a few years. In succeeding
years there would be no hideous spectres of want
to disturb his dream of ease. Even the farm
hand received good pay; and with steady employment and little expense, for his wants were
few, he could look forward to the not far distant day when he would be on an equal footing
with his employer.

In 1866 wheat sold at $2.19, corn at 68 cents,
oats at 50 cents, rye at $1.19, barley at $1.00,

potatoes at 68 cents, buckwheat at 97 cents and
hay at $14.50 per ton. The prices of different
articles varied with the season; but the above list
is a pretty fair average of ruling prices for a
long period. In 1895 the prevailing prices for
above articles were: Wheat 50 cents, corn 25
cents, oats 19 cents, rye 44 cents, barley 33
cents, potatoes 26 cents and hay $8.35 per ton.
In the following year prices were still lower, ex-
cepting for wheat, which arose in price in the
late fall on account of the failure of the crop in
India.

With the prices of thirty years ago for his
produce the farmer could live in comfort, could
pay for his farm, could allow his children, in the
winter season at least, to enjoy the advantages
of higher education offered by the towns, and
could indulge in many of the luxuries of life.
When this fundamental and most extensive
branch of industry was in a prosperous condition,
it stimulated trade in every other class of mechanical and manufacturing labor. The farmer
could afford to buy more and better clothes for
his family, he could have better buildings and

more costly furniture for his home, and could have better stock and implements for his farm. As a necessary sequence all this included a greater demand for the product of the loom, more work for the carpenter, the painter, the cabinet maker and allied trades, and more money to expend on many little luxuries of various kinds. The farms through New York State will average over ninety acres, and in the season of high prices the income of the farmer should range from $1,200 to $2,000 a year; but with this income diminished one-half, or two-thirds, by low prices, the farmer must exercise economy to live; and dependent branches of trade will suffer depression from his loss.

The annual products of the average farm in the United States should be sufficient to support a family in comfort and even luxury. In France there are over 5,000,000 leasers and owners of land engaged in cultivating the soil, and these farms average less than ten* acres; yet France is the most prosperous country in the world. Why is not prosperity the reward of the

*Eight and three-fourths acres. (Leslie).

American farmer? For many years, notwithstanding the capital invested, his income has not
exceeded that of the common laborer with no
capital but his strong arms, or perhaps, a shovel.

The population of the state has about doubled
in twenty years; railroads have been built
through the land, bringing the farms closer to
the markets; wealth and the demand for food
products have enormously increased in the same
period. Improvements in farm implements
have kept pace with the progress in every other
branch of industry. Every farmer has his mowing machines, his reaper and binder, his patent
drill and sower, to enable him to increase his
crops and lessen his expense.

In the large farms of the West and the South,
steam is utilized to draw the plows, to reap the
harvest and to thrash the grain. "The biggest
wheat harvester in the world is in use for the
first time on Robert Island, in the San Juaquin
river near Stockton, California. This machine
has a cutting line of fifty-two feet, and it also
'threshes and sacks the grain. This it does at the
rate of three sixty-pound sacks of wheat every

minute. In one run around a field of 4,000
acres it will turn out many sacks of wheat ready
for the market. It has reduced the cost of harvesting to a minimum, and the number of days
consumed in getting a large field ready for market will be about half that of the regular harvester. Eight or ten men handle it easily, while
it is turning out from 1,500 to 1,800 sacks a day
of ten hours, and sweeping 100 acres of grain
clean. No difficulty has been experienced in
harvesting, as the traction engine, which was
built especially for the machine, pushes it
through the thick grain with about the same
ease that an ordinary engine would draw a wagon
over a country road. A general employment of
these machines in all the great grain fields of the
northwestern and the Pacific slope states, will
enable American wheat growers to lead all other
nations in the production of that great staple of
commerce."*

Twenty years ago all this work was done by
hand. Five or six men were employed in the
planting season, where but one or two are re-

*New York Paper.

quired at present. Scores of men filled the harvest fields, for five or six weeks at very high wages, to mow the hay and reap the grain. At early morning the men went forth with their scythe or their sickle to labor long and hard it is true, but joyfully, for the reward sweetened their labor. Two or three men to supplement the work of machines are all that are needed now to do the work of the scores of harvesters of former years. The click and hum of steel have driven out the merry laugh, the jest and jibe, of the toilers of former days.

The farming population has not increased in the same proportion as the towns, notwithstanding all these improvements, and very many good farms in our most populous states* have been abandoned because not sufficiently remunerative to sustain an ordinary family.

In 1790 one-thirtieth of the population of the United States lived in cities of 8,000 or more inhabitants. In 1880 the proportion of city dwellers had increased to nearly one-fourth of the

*There are many abandoned farms in the central part of New York.

whole. The population of the State of New York has about doubled in forty years, from 1850 to 1890, but the population of the cities has multiplied from four to ten times in the same period.

The wheat production of New York State had fallen from 1870 to 1890 from 12,178,462 to 8,304,539 bushels, whilst the wheat yield of the entire country had nearly doubled in the same time. The farms of New York are close to the center of population of the country, and are within easy reach of the great marts and the food consuming regions of the world, yet they cannot compete in grain raising with the great farms of the far distant North West. The cost of transportation from these farms to the seaboard, or through the milling centers to the markets, is very great, but the immense quantity produced at a diminished cost through the use of machinery, makes grain raising in the West a profitable business.

The quantity of wheat raised in the Dakotas alone increased from 170,662 bushels in 1870 to 42,944,503 bushels in 1890, whilst the popu-

lation of this region increased only from 14,189
to 511.527, in the same period. The wheat
yield had multipiled itself over 250 times in
twenty years, whilst the population of the territory had multiplied itself but about thirty-five
times.

Tho number of large farms has greatly increased in recent years. Within the last census
decade, from 1880 to 1890, the number of farms
containing between 500 and 1,000 acres has increased over eleven per cent., whilst 2,968 farms
of 1,000 or more acres were enumerated. One
farm in the South West, which was formed within the above period, contains upwards of 1,500,-
000 acres. All the cultivating on this immense
farm is done by steam power. A large tract, say
half a mile wide, is taken, and an engine is placed
at either side. These engines are portable, and
operate cables attached to plows. Three men
under this system can plow thirty acres of land in
a single day. The harrowing and planting of
different kinds are done in a similar manner.
There are great farms in the North West which
are operated on a like gigantic scale, the level

prairie land being peculiarly adapted to this form of farming.

These great farms of the West, which have been called "Bonanza Farms," began about 1875. Before that time it would have been a risky business venture to attempt to cultivate thousands of acres with uncertain and high-priced labor, and with an inconstant and vacillating market. About the year 1875 mowing machines, labor-saving reapers and cultivators began to be extensively employed on farms, displacing a vast number of men, thus making the management of large farms not only possible, but also very profitable. With a foreman and two or three men, and a full supply of labor-saving machines, a doctor or a lawyer could pursue his profession in the city and operate a vast farm in the grain belt. A knowledge of farming was not necessary. It was sufficient to know that it was a very profitable investment, which would yield from fifty to 500 per cent. I have known a railroad conductor in the State of New York to run an extensive wheat farm in Dakota, by merely taking a pleasant trip of a few weeks, twice a year to his farm to see that the grain was sowed, and the harvest gathered, threshed and sold. These farms are owned by men in England, in Ireland and in different parts of the Eastern states. They can be run at a fair profit with wheat at twenty-five cents a bushel, and collosal fortunes must be made for their owners when wheat commands seventy or more cents in the market.

The small farmer cannot compete with these extensive enterprises, and they are forced from the field, or are compelled to limit their labors to branches of farming where less capital is required, but where more skill and more hands are necessary to carry on the work.

The great Bonanza Farms of the West have but very slightly lessened the cost of flour to the retail buyer, when we take into account the greatly reduced cost of production. Flour sold at seven dollars a barrel, in the small towns in Dakota, when wheat was worth seventy cents a bushel. Nor have these great farms contributed to a rise in wages or perceptibly increased the demand for labor. Laborers in the Bonanza Farm region are very irregularly employed at a very low average pay. Not one of the Bonanza Farms has a permanent dwelling and the full complement of men are necessary for only two or three months in the year, and even during this season the most unskilled labor is capable of doing the work. This labor may be obtained in the market actually cheaper than slave labor; because the employer of free unskilled labor may employ and discharge men at will, and may engage labor for only the busy season, whereas, the slave owner is obliged to maintain his slaves during the entire year.

Cheap labor brings degradation and decline to the nation, whilst a high rate of wages leads on prosperity in its train.* The nations are so closely bound together in their commercial relations that the prosperity or depression of one contributes to the prosperity or works the ruin of many others; and the "pauper labor" of Europe is finding its counterpart in the pauperized labor of the United States.

In plowing, one man with improved machines can do the work that was formerly done by more

*Adam Smith.

than a score of men. Until recently grain was sown by hand. A man would carry a pouch or sack suspended from his shoulder, and with measured tread would walk through the field sowing his seed; now a boy seated upon the latest improved sower will do ten times the amount of work with ease. In corn planting the cultivator displaces twenty men, and in gathering the ripened ear machines do the work of half a score; whilst in shelling corn, one man can now do the work of one hundred or more working in the old way.

Reapers came into use early in the present century; but it was only within the past decade that they attained their fullest development, and now one man with the latest style of reaper can do the same amount of work that was formerly done by three hundred men with sickles .

Threshing the sheaves of ripened grain on the barn floor with flails gave healthful employment to many men throughout the winter season; now the dusty, noisy, man devouring steam thresher does the same amount of work in two or three days.

There are labor-saving machines for gathering and for shelling the corn, which displace from ten to one hundred and fifty men.

When the grain is brought to the mill to be ground into flour the labor-saving principle still prevails.   Mills can now, with the assistance of two or three men, turn out 1,000 barrels of flour in the same length of time that they could mill twenty or thirty barrels under the old process.

Feudalism in Europe favored large landed estates and vassalage of the peasantry.   The struggle for liberty implied also, either directly or as a corollary, peasant proprietorship in land. The advance of civilization in every country was attended by increased numbers of individual owners of land, and the great majority of culti- vated soil in every civilized country is held by small proprietors.   Individual liberty would naturally assert itself in the right to independent ownership.   Small holdings of land seem pecu- liarly adapted to prosperity.   There is then no necessity for labor-saving machinery on the farm to supplant the toiler; easily attained ownership through small holdings offers a larger field for employment, and a higher state of cultivation creates a greater demand for the various forms of manufacture.

Napoleon rendered facile the transfer of titles to land; then he divided the vast estates into small holdings, and in this way he laid the foundation of **prosperity** in France. Statistics prove that the **most prosperous** provinces in France are those in which there are the greatest number of small proprietors. Work is plentiful and wages are high, results which invariably follow from increased demands, and a great stimulus is given to every line of industry by the healthful tone of the primary calling. Farming on an extensive scale would necessarily involve not only **large** outlay, but also great indebtedness; yet all these are supposed to be offset by vastly increased resources and returns. Investigation, however, proves that the large farms are not only heavily encumbered, but in almost all countries that they have more than their proportionate share of indebtedness .

Farming in the United States, under present conditions, is a very unprofitable occupation.

The only farm that pays is the Bonanza Grain Farm, or the cattle ranch. Men of means, from present indications, will, in the future, invest in one of these two methods as the only profitable forms of farming. As in all other branches of industry, there is in farming a tendency towards centralization of production.

"That the only possible future for agriculture, prosecuted for the sake of producing the great staples of food, is to be found in large farms, worked with ample capital, especially in the form of machinery, and with labor organized somewhat after the factory system, is coming to be the opinion of many of the best authorities, both in the United States and Europe."*

With the growth and extension of these machine-worked and factory-formed farms, agriculture as an occupation for the small farmer will cease to offer profitable employment, except in the form of small truck or poultry farms near the large markets.

The highest good of the greatest number was formerly supposed to constitute the fundamental

*"Recent Economic Changes." (D. A. Wells).

principle of national prosperity, but the fin de
siecle trend is towards the highest good of the
smallest number; and this tendency is indirectly
advocated by political economists of high standing as the progress of civilization. No nation
ever has been or ever will be prosperous and
happy unless the great mass of people obtain
work at fair wages.*

Something is wrong in the system when a
farmer in the United States cannot make a living
on fifty or one hundred acres of land. The products of agriculture here are enormous; depression could never be traced to a general failure of
crops. This country not only produces enough
to feed and clothe her own inhabitants, but ships
are continually bearing her products to every
country in the world, where a market can be
found, and the only limit to her exports is the
absence of demand. In twenty-five years, from
1860 to 1885, the exports of agricultural products from the United States have more than

*"Cheap labor means degradation of the nation;
dear labor means prosperity." Adam Smith).

doubled in value.* About 100,000,000 bushels
of wheat are annually shipped from the United
States to Europe, and much more could be sent
if there were a greater demand; but our wheat
there meets a sharp competition in the product
of India, which finds an easy approach to Europe through the Suez Canal. United States
consuls and exporters of grain hope to find a new
market for our wheat in the ports of China and
Japan.

A short time ago there was an almost universal cry for the protection of American labor
against the pauper labor of Europe; yet here are
our noble American farmers competing in the
markets of the world with the Coolie labor of
India and China, the cheapest and most debased
on the globe.

A little reflection upon the facts here pre-

*From 256,000,000 in 1860 to 530,000,000 in 1885.
In May, 1897, Russell Sage, who is president of the
Iowa Central R. R., received a letter from one of
the Railroad Commissioners of Iowa, asking him
to make a cheap rate on corn, so that farmers
could ship it out of the state. It was rotting, but
present prices would not pay farmers to haul it.
In fifteen years the production of corn had ex-
panded from 5,000,000 to 300,000,000 bushels.—New
York Herald, May 16, 1897.

sented will convince any unprejudiced mind that the introduction of labor-saving machinery in the work of the farm, has brought about this condition of things, has made farm life in America unprofitable, and has reduced the noble and independent American farmer to a condition of helpless poverty, where even vassalage to a mighty lord might be welcomed as a boon to his hopeless state. Labor-saving machinery might have been directed towards improving the condition of the farmer, and might have been made to bear the burdens of toil; but the greed of men has made them instruments of depression and a curse to the land.

In the last forty years the products of agriculture have increased more than four-fold, whilst the population has increased only about three times. In twenty years, from 1870 to 1890, the acreage under cultivation in the United States has nearly doubled, but the value of the products of the farm has scarcely changed. In 1870 these were valued at $2,447,000,000, whilst in 1890 they had only increased to $2,460,000,000.

In 1840, when the population of the United States was 17,069,453, over 3,700,000 people were employed in agricultural pursuits out of a total of 4,796,407 employed; and their comfortable homes, their well kept farms, the well groomed stock, the independent air of the farmer, were proofs positive that farming was a profitable calling.

There was a ready market for their produce, and a good price for their goods. In 1890 out of a total population of over 62,000,000, about 8,300,000 were engaged in the same industry. The ratio of increase of agricultural products for many years had far exceeded the increase of population; yet the ratio of those employed in this pursuit to the total employed had greatly decreased. The markets are overstocked; prices fall; weeds grow in the fields where wheat should bloom; homes are abandoned; decay and neglect mark the desolation wrought in agriculture by the introduction of the new economy of labor-saving machines, which displace the farmer and the farm hand, and force them into other industries, if they can find work, or into the ranks of the great and ever increasing army of the unemployed in the cities and towns, into degradation and want.

Over 100,000 were displaced in twenty years, from 1861 to 1881, in England by the introduction of labor-saving agricultural machines. These were forced from the fields to the cities and towns, into the prisons or poor houses.

Golden harvests may still fill the land with plenty, but they are no longer a symbol of the rich reward for invested capital and expended labor.

The amount of wheat raised in the State of New York had not perceptibly changed in twenty-five years, from 1867 to 1892; but the vast difference in value shows very forcibly the immense loss of profit in the farming industry. In 1867 the wheat crop of New York State was 8,250,000 bushels; and in 1892 the crop had increased by 150,000 bushels, making a total of 8,405,000 bushels. The value of this wheat crop in 1867 was $21,780,000; but in 1892, twenty-five years later, when the crop had increased by 150,000 bushels, the value had decreased to less than one-third of 1867 value, being only $7,144,385.*

There is a disposition to lay the blame for over-production of agricultural, as well as manufacturing products and consequent industrial depression, upon immigration; for in this manner the market is over supplied with cheap labor, wages are lowered, competition for employment increased, the consuming power is crippled and "hard times" follow.

This is a very plausible but false reasoning. From 1880 to 1890 "the South"** enjoyed a decade of prosperity (judged from the amount of her products) unexcelled in the history of nations. There was no foreign cheap labor to compete with the native element in the home market; and the enormous increase in manufacturing, mining and agricultural products should have created an extraordinary demand for labor of all kinds, and should have vastly increased the rate of wages.

*Bureau of Statistics of Labor, 1892.
**Texas is not included in the Southern states, because it has peculiar characteristics.

In 1890 only two per cent. of the total population of fourteen Southern states was foreign born; and the rate of increase of population for the decade was only 17.3 per cent., the lowest, with one exception, on record. During this period the two Southern states, whose population increased at the highest rate, are also the two states in which manufacturing industry is least developed; and the three largest manufacturing states of "the South" show the lowest rate of increase of population.*

The average rate of wages paid in these fourteen Southern states, in 1866, was $18.18 per month; in 1882 the rate had gone down to $15.78; and in the following decade it undulated slightly each year until it settled at $15.99 in 1892.

There was no influx of foreign cheap labor during this period to crowd out the skilled high-priced native; yet wages decreased whilst products in all branches of industry attained an abnormal growth. The value of the total products of the textile industries in the United

*Bureau of Statistics of Labor, New York, 1892.

States in 1880 was $500,376,068, and in 1890 this arose to $693,048,702, an increase of about thirty-seven per cent. The value of all the products of the manufacturing industries in the United States in 1880 was computed at $5,849,-191,458; and in 1890 this had increased to $9,056,765,996, an increase of over sixty-nine per cent. During this same decade the value of products of manufacture in the fourteen Southern States had arisen from about $500,000,000 to over $1,000,000,000;* had increased over 100 per cent., whilst the population had increased but a little over seventeen per cent.

Judging from the enormous increase in the manufacturing industries in the south during this decade, we might imagine that people had abandoned the farms for the factories; yet we find that in the same period agricultural products had increased in volume and diversity at a similar prodigious rate. Agricultural products were diversified, and new lines were added which offered prompt returns for facile effort. Factories for making butter and cheese were started

*Eleventh Census,

all over the South during this decade, and practically opened a new and extensive field of industry through the entire region. The amount of milk sent to butter and cheese factories had increased in this decade from five to over 100 times in quantity. In Louisiana the quantity increased from one-quarter million gallons to twelve million gallons; and in Alabama the amount increased from one-quarter to fifty-five million gallons; and in the other states the ratio of increase varied between the above amounts.

The quantities of poultry and eggs placed on the market during this decade had also increased in all the Southern states at a very remarkable rate, being slightly above the ratio of increase for the United States. The output of sugar and molasses in the South had more than doubled in this decade; and the tonnage of hay had multiplied itself many times.

There was no great influx of foreign population to assist in this enormously increased production; and even the ratio of increase of the native population was far below the normal; but into every class of productive industry had been introduced the labor-saving machines, which render men, except as consumers, useless articles in the world.

The South had abundance of food products raised upon her own soil to supply her people before 1880, but increased facilities of transportation and prospective wealth lured her into sending her products to the markets of the world. She produced far more than she could consume, and her enormously increased production led economic theorists to look upon this period as one of most wonderful prosperity. She did not add to the comfort, prosperity or happiness of a largely increased population within her borders; but she added to the wealth of a few—and this is progress, according to the standard of fin de siecle wisdom.

Civilization is wealth, according to nineteenth century philosophy; and men—the proletariat—are only the instruments used in its production.

CHAPTER II.

SHOEMAKING.

With their broad expanse of territory, with their millions upon millions of fertile acres, with their rich rolling prairies; with the pleasing climate of the South and Southwest, and with the eager air and exhilerating atmosphere of the North, the United States must return agriculture as the chief industry of the people for many years to come. Close to farming, which supplies food for the millions, come in rank the great trades which supply covering, comfort and protection for the body. The votaries of Crispin some years ago could be counted by the millions, and according to the census of 1860, the greatest number of men employed in any one industry after agriculture, were those engaged in making shoes.

From the time that man first sought covering for his feet to protect them from rude contact with the earth to the present day, the skill and ingenuity of those following the trade of Crispin have been employed to perfect the art. The

first forms of the art were probably mere soles
made of wood, of cloth, of hides of animals, or
of metal, which were fastened to the feet with
thongs. As each successive generation profited
by the inventions and experience of their fore-
fathers, progress was made through the sandal,
the rough and ungainly forms of boots, to the
comfortable elegance and perfection of the art
attained in the nineteenth century. The old
Roman patrician was distinguished in rank
from the plebeian order by his footwear as well
as by his toga, and every century since has witnessed some effort to indicate the social strata
by the covering of the feet. The Roman patrician not only had fine material for his footgear,
but wore it higher up the leg than did the plebeian, and some of the former even wore shoes
or sandals with soles of gold. All through the
centuries the proper clothing of the feet has
been an important art, and vast numbers have
been employed in every age to supply mankind
with the varying styles.

Before 1846, when the Howe sewing machine
was patented, most of the boots and shoes

brought into existence throughout the world were made in the old way, by men who had spent years of apprenticeship in learning the trade, sitting upon benches and holding the leather upon a last. This art is not entirely lost; for the finest boots and shoes of the day are still made in this manner, but the vast majority of the goods are made in the modern factory. In the old way one man, with such implements as were in use, could make a pair of ordinary shoes in two days; and with repairing and mending he might be able to keep one hundred people comfortably clad during the year. This proportion throughout the whole country would give employment, every day in the year, to 700,-000 men to furnish the people of the United States with the customary covering for the feet.

The application of machinery has wrought a most wonderful revolution in the shoemaking industry. Rude attempts were made in England in the past century to construct a machine which would supplant manual labor in sewing shoes. There was no appreciable displacement of labor, however, in this department until the sewing machine was fitted for this grade of work. With the Goodyear sewing machine one man can now sew as many shoes in a day as eight men could in the old way.* Every distinguishable part of the boot or shoe has a separate department in the modern factory, and especially invented machines do the work that was formerly done by hand. There are machines for cutting, and machines for rounding soles; there are machines for shaving or trimming heels, machines for skiving or shaving uppers, an adaptation of the sewing machine for closing the uppers, and a machine for sewing these on to the soles; machines for attaching the heels; machines for pegging, where these are used; machines for finishing the soles. There are machines for every conceivable branch of the industry; and these machines require very little guidance from man to perfect their work, whilst some work automatically, merely requiring a fresh supply of material at stated intervals.

In the work of sewing shoes one man, with modern methods and improved machinery, can

*Report of the Commissioner of Labor, 1886.

now turn out 250 pairs a day, doing the work
that would require the labor of eight men, by
the old method, to accomplish in the same time.
With the McKay machine one man can now
handle 300 pairs a day, whereas, formerly five
pairs would constitute a day's labor. In nailing
on heels one man, with modern machinery, can
now do as much work as five men could formerly
do, without machinery, in the old way.

Many of these labor-saving machines do not
require the attention or guidance of skilled
artisans, or even the developed intelligence or
the physical power of men; but women and even
children operate these voiceless automatons that
deprive the American mechanic of his (God-
given and constitutionally- guaranteed) heritage.

In 1850, according to the census, 105,253
persons were employed in the manufacture of
boots and shoes. The factory system of making
shoes was even at that early date in operation,
and 32,948 persons of the above number were
females engaged in this department of labor.
The value of the product in this branch of industry was estimated at $53,967,408. Ten years

later the number of operatives had only increased to 127,427, whilst the value of the products had almost doubled. In 1890 the number of employees reported in this line of industry was 139,333 in the factories, and 35,448 engaged in custom work and repairing, whilst the
value of the product of the factories had risen to
the enormous sum of $220,649,358. Here we
see the enormously increased productive power
of the operative with the aid of improved labor-
saving machinery. The productive power of
the operative had increased four-fold, whilst the
number employed had only increased by about
one-third.

Not only are shoes enough made to supply the
demand of the millions in this land, but manufacturers are seeking foreign markets for their
goods; and already a large trade in American
made shoes has been built up in England, where
the superior quality of these goods commands a
ready sale. In some of the British provinces
fully one-half of the shoes used are made in the
United States.

From census returns it would seem that the

employees had benefited by the vastly increased per capita production. In 1860 the average yearly wages of the employee was estimated to be $247, for the different grades of labor and the different sexes. In 1890 the wages had risen to $483 per capita, according to the census returns. This would seem to indicate a very gratifying betterment in the condition of the shoe factory employee, and a disposition of the employer to share some of the immensely increased profits of capital with labor. Unfortunately this seeming increase in the wages of employees is not real. The different methods employed in taking the census at different periods, and the different systems used in the classification of employees, make these figures very unreliable. In the census of 1890, under the head of employees of the shoe factories were placed all the office help, the superintendents and managers, and even the officers of the company, with the possible exception of the president and directors. Those engaged in custom work, and repairing, have been able to earn a fair compensation for their skill and labor. The 36,000 occupied in this branch

of the business report net earnings of over $16,-
000,000; and when we reflect that many of these
are unskilled cobblers, it is evident that skilled
workmen in the higher grades of custom work
still command good wages.

The operatives in shoe factories are not so
fortunately situated in regard to wages as the
figures above cited would seem to indicate; for
nearly a decade has elapsed since those statistics
were gathered, and they were misleading, as we
have seen, even when they were compiled.

One of the old style shoemakers recently told
the writer that twenty years ago the journeyman
shoemaker was as much a prince as the plumber
is today. Then ten or twelve dollars was not
an exorbitant price for a pair of shoes. When
a man wanted his shoes heeled and tapped he
paid two dollars and a half, and he did not consider this too much. Now, the manufacturers
pay on an average twelve or fifteen cents for
making a pair of shoes, and they even strive to
cut down this paltry sum.

The shoe factory is a comparatively modern* institution; and it is only within the past two or three years that labor-saving machinery has been introduced into some of the departments of this industry. Buttonholes were made by hand up to three years ago; and then the ubiquitous labor-saving machine invaded this branch of shoemaking, and relegated the well-paid workmen to other fields of labor. Shoemaking, like all the other branches of industry into which labor-saving machinery has been introduced, has suffered depression from the enormous output of cheap products. The profits of the manufacturers may have been enormous in the early years of the factory system of shoemaking; but competition and the increasing cost of placing their goods on the market have forced many of them from the field.

As in every other branch of productive industry into which labor-saving machinery has been introduced, the shoe market has been glutted. Manufacturers are seeking foreign

*Shoe factories came into existence about 1866. (Carrol D. Wright).

markets for their goods, because they can undersell European makers on account of their
cheaper methods of production. Large fortunes
were made in this business before overproduction gave rise to sharp competition, and competition forced manufacturers to reduce prices to
obtain a market for their goods.

What great boon has been conferred upon humanity by the modern economical system of
making shoes in factories with the aid of labor-
saving machinery? The producing power per
capita of employees has been increased four-fold
in forty years,* and a great quantity of goods
has been put upon the market at a greatly reduced cost of production. Who has reaped the
benefit of this so-called progress; are factory-
made shoes any better than the hand-made custom goods? They are not so good; and no one
ever made such claim for them. Are they
cheaper? They probably cost less to the buyer
than the hand-made shoe; but they are not so
well made as the latter; are not so neat; will not

*In 1850 the value of products per capita of em-
ployees was $417, and in 1890 it was $1,583. (Census).

wear so well; and in the end are fully as expensive, considering the grade of goods, as the hand-made article. A great quantity of inferior goods has been placed upon the market, which will shrink and collapse when they are thoroughly soaked with rain.

Formerly when the apprentice learned his trade he could, in a short time, start a little shop of his own, for much capital was not required in this business; and with frugality and industry he could make a very comfortable living. Variety of labor relieved the monotony of toil; and the jibe and jest of fellow laborer or friend made pleasant the hours of this independent life. Now the business is transferred to the stuffy shop, and the hum of the machine has replaced the cheery voice of man. Humdrum sameness has supplanted skillful and diversified work, and the operatives become like machines—little more useful and capable than those run by steam.

Humanity in general has derived no benefit from the change from an old style of small independent shops and hand-made goods to the modern factory where machine-made shoes are turned out by the thousands. Those engaged in this work as employees have not been benefited. Their wages are less than they would be under the old system; their work is not so pleasant. Employers and capitalists must reap the immense profit there should be in the industry.

The principal effect of the factory system of making shoes upon those engaged in this industry as workers, has been to lower the wages of the few remaining; to substitute children and women for men; and to cast half a million of men out of a profitable calling and force them to join their disinherited brothers from the farm. And this is fin de siecle progress; this is civilization!

These economic methods of making boots and shoes are not confined to the United States, but, like an evil contagion, have spread through parts of Europe. In March, 1895, ten thousand operatives in shoe factories of London went on a strike against the introduction of improved labor-saving machinery from America. At Leicester some 30,000 more operatives joined in the protest with their brothers from London. All throughout the kingdom men went on strike; but what avail? Thousands of men were forced out of other employment by labor-saving machinery, and were ready to take the place of the strikers. The poor idle operatives could see the bread taken from their mouths, and from the mouths of their wives and children, and could only cry out in feeble protest.

And Yankee ingenuity continues its triumphant career of pauperizing the world!

CHAPTER III.

CLOTH AND CLOTHING.

Closely allied to the shoemaking industry are the cloth and clothing making trades.

Prior to the Revolution all the cloth manufactured in the United States was made by hand. Every well regulated farm house had its spining wheel and its hand loom, and here the women of the house spun the wool and wove the cloth that made comfortable clothes for the members of the household. When sheep were numerous there was a superfluity of wool and this could be sold in its raw shape, or made into cloth and sold in the village stores, or bartered in the towns for luxuries which the farm could not provide.

England enjoyed for many years a monopoly in the cloth market, because she possessed valuable machinery which enabled her to produce at little cost. She would not allow any of this machinery to be exported, so that she might maintain her supremacy in this branch of trade. England did not, however, long precede the United

States in the use of machinery for the manufacture of cloth; for it was not until 1760 that a machine was invented for spinning cotton, and the year 1785 witnessed the first operation of the power loom.   In 1786, the Massachusetts Legislature offered $1,000 to the inventor of a machine for carding and spinning wool, and a short time after an expert from England, who had been an operative in his native land, came to the United States, and, with the aid of Yankee ingenuity, machines were made which enabled this country to compete with Europe in the manufacture of cloth.

Before the machines for carding and spinning were extensively used, and before the factory system was established, these branches of cloth making were carried on by hand in the towns and gave employment to a large number of men. So necessary was the cloth making industry that every family in Massachusetts Bay Colony was ordered by the General Court to spin ninety pounds a year, under penalty of twelve shillings for each pound short.   Land was freely given to skilled weavers from England or Germany on condition that they would ply their vocation in the interest of the town. Cotton was imported from the West India Islands, and the growth of hemp and flaxseed and the raising of sheep was urged as a public necessity.

Women very rarely worked for wages* before the rise of the factory system. The young women, whose parents lived on farms, had plenty of work to keep them busy at home. These were the days before the advent of the modern labor-saving, pauper-making sewing machine, when cloth and clothing making required an immense number of hands. Girls then were not looking for clerkships at starvation wages, nor were they invading fields sacred to the male callings, and forcing men out of profitable employment, for they had abundance of work at home. Girls with homes could not be allured into domestic service, and the only ones who could be pressed into this line of work were con-

*The statement, sometimes found in works on political economy and industrial questions, of the increased per cent. of the employed in recent years, is very misleading. Those engaged in home duties were not classed as employed.

victs, or what were called "Redemptioners,"* principally from England. Slaves and Indians were occasionally forced into service, and the house was fortunate indeed that had an adequate supply of domestic help.

The old system of hand manufacture promoted the prosperity of small towns, and favored their establishment and growth at relatively close intervals through the settled portions of the land. This gave the farmer a home market for his surplus wool, and the clothing makers found a convenient trade with the townspeople for their goods.

In the olden days an average hand-loom weaver could turn out from forty-two to forty-eight yards of common shirting in a week.** With the power looms of today one weaver could produce at least 2,000 yards a week. Since 1813 there has been a continual improvement in machinery for the manufacture of all grades of cloth. The principal, and in many cases the

*These were paupers who sold their services for a certain period in payment of their passage.
**Commissioner of Labor Report, 1886.

only, aim in these improvements has been to increase the amount of production and to decrease the cost; and as labor is one of the greatest items of cost in production, the tendency of inventions has been to substitute machines for the hands of men.

There seems to be no limit to the improvement of machinery, and consequently to the displacement of labor. In weaving cotton goods of a fair quality, a weaver with a hand loom could formerly weave from sixty to eighty picks a minute; a power loom will now weave near two hundred picks a minute of the same quality cloth. It is not alone in the increased productive power of the individual machine that progress has been made, but the machines have been so constructed that they require less attention from the operative, and instead of one loom requiring the individual care of the weaver the latter may now run from four to ten looms, according to the quality of cloth With the single spindle, hand wheel, one spinner could spin about five hanks of No. 32 twist in a week. One spinner now with a pair of self-acting mules, of over two thousand spindles, with the assistance of two boys, can produce over fifty-five thousand hanks of No. 32 twist in the same time. "It is quite generally agreed that there has been a displacement, taking all processes of cotton manufacture into consideration, in the proportion of three to one."*

In a mill in Philadelphia, in July 1877, a calculation was made of the displacement of labor by new spinning devices, and the remarkable discovery was made that one hundred and fifty-one persons could spin as much yarn, with the latest labor-saving machinery, as one hundred thousand women could spin in the same time, in the old way.**   In the manufacture of woolen goods there was a displacement of ninety-eight per cent. in ten years, from 1865 to 1875;*** and every decade of the present century has witnessed the substitution of machines for men in the manufacture of cloth.   And yet the cause of "hard times," of the industrial depression, is

*Commissioner of Labor Report.

**Moody.   The Industrial Problem.

***Report of Massachusetts State Bureau.

an inexplicable mystery to our wise men! At the present day one girl, with up-to-date machinery, can make three hundred yards of cloth in a day, where formerly three yards would constitute a fair day's work.

With the increase of population there should be proportionate increase of consumption of products, and there must, consequently, be an increase of supply to correspond with the demand. From 1830 to 1860, the number of spindles in the cotton mills increased from 1,246,703 to 5,235,727; and the number of looms had increased from 33,433 to 126,313 in the same period.* The capital invested in this branch of manufacture had increased from $40,612,984 to $98,585,267, in the same period of thirty years. The spindles and the looms had quadrupled, whilst the capital employed had but little more than doubled. More capital is necessary to manufacture with labor-saving machinery, but

*"Industrial Evolution in United States." (Wright.)

the profit is proportionately greater because the pay roll is far smaller.*

The population of the United States had grown in the same thirty years, from 1830 to 1860, from a little less than thirteen millions to about thirty-one millions. The population had little more than doubled whilst the product of cotton and wool textile products had increased from about thirty-one millions, in 1840, to upwards of one hundred and eighty millions in 1860; the products had increased over six-fold. From 1860 to 1890, the population of the United States just about doubled in numbers; but the textile products in cotton and wool had grown in the same period from $188,000,000 to over $538,000,000; they had increased in value three-fold whilst the population doubled. doubled.

From 1850 to 1890, employees in the textile industries had increased 248.47 per cent. and the

*In forty years, from 1850 to 1890, the ratio of capital employed to value of products had but slightly changed. In 1850 capital was $112,513,057, and value of products, $128,769,971; in 1890 these were: capital $739,893,661, and value of products, $821,946,262. (Eleventh Census of United States).

value of products had increased 460.65 per cent. in the same period; and this difference in the percentage of increase of employees and products represents the displacement of labor by machinery. In 1850, in the combined textile industries in the United States, 146,897 persons were employed, and in 1890 this number had increased to 571,897.

The amount of wages paid employees at the different periods is not so easily ascertained on account of the different methods employed in gathering statistics for the census. In 1850 the wages were not reported. In 1860 the total wages paid was $40,353,462, an average of $208 per employee. In 1870 this had increased to $315 per employee. In 1880 the average was $293 for each person. In 1890 the average wages had arisen to $349 for each person employed. At first sight this would seem to indicate a handsome increase in wages, and would give evidence of improvement in the condition of the toiler; but figures are sometimes misleading. In the census of 1890, all the officers and clerks of the manufactories were classed as employees, and their high salaries helped to swell the list of wages. The number of children employed, whose wages were necessarily small, had greatly decreased on account of factory laws, and this added greatly to the average wages. Taking all things into consideration, the wages reported in the eleventh census for employees of textile goods do not show any advance over the wages of 1870.

Inventions and improvements for lowering the cost of production have been eagerly sought and more generally applied since the statistics for the last census were gathered. It is a curious fact, well known to those familiar with patents that depressed periods often result in the stimulation of invention.* From 500 to 5,000 patents are issued every year at Washington; and many of these are designed to displace labor, and consequently, to lower the cost of production.

The present producing facilities of the textile manufactories in the United States are so great that, no doubt, they could readily supply the

*"Industrial Evolution in the United States." (Carroll D. Wright.)

market by working one-half, or even one-fourth time; and where the supply so far exceeds the demand competition for the market must be very sharp, forcing the manufacturer into methods of economy in production. There are many manufacturers, no doubt, who would be delighted to pay their employees better wages under more favorable conditions; but there are very few in the textile or any other industry for charity; and in competition with others in the same business, they must adopt the latest and best methods for making money. One manufacturer cannot afford to cling to the old hand-work system, employing very large numbers of skilled men at high wages, whilst his neighbor in the same business adopts the latest style of labor-saving machinery, which may be run by children or cheap labor, thus reducing the element of cost to a minimum. But, if all manufacturers were obliged, by law, to eliminate the labor-saving machines from their works and return to the old methods of hand work and skilled labor, the system would place all on equal footing, and should be satisfactory to all. It would

cost the manufacturer more to place his goods
on the market; but these would command a better price; the market would be enlarged, because
this system would increase the consuming
powers of the skilled laborers of the land by giving them more work and better wages.

With the growth of the textile industry one
would suppose that factories would follow the
increase of population, and that works would be
started in the new towns and cities of the land.
The contrary has been the case; the tendency
has been to centralize all the different branches
of the textile industry, and a few towns manufacture nearly the entire product.   Philadelphia
is the centre of the wool manufacture; Fall
River, Mass., is the centre of the cotton manufacture; Patterson, N. J., makes nearly all the
silk goods; and Cohoes, N. Y., has a monopoly
of the hosiery and knit goods.   It is somewhat
remarkable that, in forty years, the number of
establishments engaged in the textile manufacture, has not increased over twenty-five per cent.,
although the value of their output has increased
about 600 per cent. in the same time.   These

mills, no doubt, have increased in size, but they have also most wonderfully increased in efficiency.

The European countries have also increased their facilities for the manufacture of textile goods; but they are more conservative over there, and they are not likely to adopt methods that will throw vast numbers of men out of employment.

Industrial depressions bear heavily on all the manufacturing countries of Europe as well as in the United States; but these periods of depression, in Europe, do not seem to be indigenous, but more of an infection caught from commercial contact with the United States. They do not experience the evil so soon; and they recover quicker from the attack .

Observant travelers in Europe, during the present depression in the United States, claim that "hard times" are not experienced in Germany or France.* Germany, according to seemingly reliable reports, has 1,000,000 textile

*Mr. L. E. Holden, proprietor Cleveland Plain-dealer; Rev. F. Elminger.

workers; yet they work overtime to supply the demand. Their wages may be small, but they live in comparative comfort, and enjoy a happy security of employment for the morrow. France continues the even tenor of her ways, and peaceful prosperity smiles upon her sunny land.

England is also comparatively free from the long continued industrial depression that has settled upon the United States: for although wages there may be somewhat lower, yet work is more steady and the cost of living is less. In the textile industries Americans turn out about twice the amount of work done by English men, for a slight increase of wages. The boss is well paid; but he is expected to "drive" things, and is responsible for the goods and the amount of work done. "The men under these bosses are poorly paid in all the Eastern states. There are many concerns where they can and do get all the help they want at eighty cents to one dollar a day."*

"Within a radius of forty-five miles from the Royal Exchange, Manchester, there is a popu-

*Bureau of Statistics of Labor. New York, 1892.

lation of 7,000,000 of people, all directly or indirectly dependent upon manufacturing. This
district enjoys a greater measure of prosperity
than any similar community in America. Those
who are able and willing to work need not
want."*

The United States has only about one-half
million people engaged in the textile factories,
yet the country is flooded with their goods, and
they are competing with European countries in
their home markets. In 1893 the United States
sent abroad 18,000 square yards of American
made carpets; and the succeeding year, 1894,
this amount had increased to 287,188 square
yards. During the month of September, 1895,
over 16,000,000 square yards of cotton cloth was
exported from the United States, to be sold in
European markets.

The great war between France and Germany,
1870 and 1871, entailed immense financial losses
upon the former country. The expense of war,
between first-class powers, is always very heavy;
but the additional burden of an enormous war

*Ibid.

indemnity would seem to be sufficient to cripple the financial resources of any land; yet strange to relate, France, the loser, paid the five milliards of francs, and the hum of industry and financial prosperity continued in the land with but slight disturbance; whilst Germany, the victor, though enriched by the war, experienced the greatest industrial disturbance in her history. The manufacturing industries of France were in a normal and healthful condition; they had not the capital to greatly increase their products, they merely aimed to supply the demand. Prior to the war Germany had not sought foreign markets, but success in war made her one of the great political powers, and she also aspired to become one of the great industrial nations of the world. The immense war indemnity had made money abundant and cheap; speculation ran riot, the industrial field, as the most profitable and most conducive to the nation's glory, was invaded by hordes of capitalists and investors; all industries were overworked, until the markets were glutted with enormous quantities of products, and excessive overproduction was felt in every branch of manufacture. German industry then almost entirely ceased until 1879, when there was a slight revival, which, however, did not last.

These cases show pretty conclusively that overproduction lies at the bottom of every industrial depression. There may be some financial disturbance which will cause a flurry; but business will soon resume its normal volume when supply and demand in products preserve their proper ratio. The great financial disturbances that have at times swept over the world like destructive simoons, have been assigned as the cause of industrial depressions but they have very little to do with them. The law of supply and demand is sovereign and absolute, and where these are normal and healthful—no overproduction or under-consumption—the financial disturbances will only affect the speculative fields which soon adjust themselves to new conditions, and the industrial and mercantile worlds will enjoy uninterrupted prosperity.

The cotton mills of New England are at present giving to the world pitiable evidence of our

crazy economic methods of production. Manufacturers claim that they cannot find markets
for their products, which are in excess of consumption, and they must cut the operatives'
wages so they can afford to wait longer for returns from their goods. The markets are flooded with the products of labor-saving machinery;
wages are near the starvation rate, yet our so-
called political economists call this mad system
progress, civilization!

The making of cloth and the cutting, fitting
and sewing of this into garments were formerly
done under one roof, and even now they are but
different branches of one great industry. Twenty
or thirty years ago the sale of ready made clothing was an infant and very insignificant industry; master and merchant tailor shops were
numerous in every town; great numbers of
skilled cutters were employed at good wages;
and the sewing of the garments by hand gave
employment to great numbers of women and
men. The better class of garments are still
made to order, because it would be very difficult to get a good fit from the ready made article.

A vast business in clothing making has sprung up in the past twenty or thirty years; and, like the factory system in cloth making, this industry has been centralized and confined to five or six cities. Some twenty or twenty-five years ago skilled tailors, including operators, pressers, basters, and button-hole makers, were capable of earning good wages, and could live in comfort and comparative luxury; but now they are the most wretched lot of human slaves to be found in America. Large numbers of them still toil, in the large cities, in "sweat shops," where they are crowded together like slaves in the galley ship, or like cattle in a car, with poor ventilation, and in these foul dens they labor twelve or fourteen, or even sixteen hours a day, when they can get work; and why? So that they may live. They are fast dying in order to live. The slaves of the South could, at least, breathe God's pure air, and they could gaze on God's blue sky; they could hear the twittering of the birds, and they could behold the beauties of nature; and they could lie down at night and sleep without the horrid spectre of starvation to haunt their

dreams. The poor garment worker hears only
the rapid whirr of the machines during the day
and the heavy rumble of the drays at night;
wearied with toil in the foul workshop he retires
to his restricted quartes in a squalid tenement
to snatch a few hours of rest before returning to
his monotonous toil. He may see the green
fields, or sniff the fresh air of lake or sea, once
or twice a year, when necessity calls, otherwise
there is no alternative but work or starve.

Thousands of men and women and girls
would leave the ranks of the poor slave garment
workers, which are already overcrowded, if
they could better their condition, but where can
they find employment that will give them bread
and soup, and a shelter? All other occupations
are crowded with able and skillful men, and
hundreds of thousands are idly waiting for some
employment that will yield the means of a respectable livelihood. All producing trades are
overcrowded, because machines are displacing
human hands. The poor tailors and garment
workers have machines also to help them in their
work. What a great blessing these labor-sav-

ing machines have been to the toilers in this trade! Do they help the poor slaves get better wages to live comfortably? No, they were not intended for that, but they help them to die easily and quickly. The foul air of the shop, the extreme heat of the pressers' work, soon fills their lungs with disease. The poor food they can afford, the scant recreation, fills their stomachs with disorders, and hastens their march to death. Most of them have families to support, and they must do this or die at once. But what are men anyway, that the world should be mindful of them? There is more money in machines in this enlightened age!

No one individual and no particular class is to blame for the present wretched state of the garment workers. There has been no deliberate attempt, or desire, on the part of the manufacturers to reduce these toilers to the verge of starvation. Their present deplorable condition is but the necessary outcome of the growth of modern industrial methods.

Twenty-five of thirty years ago nearly all the work in clothing making was done by hand.

Even those houses that dealt in ready made clothes had the garments made in their own establishments, or close at hand in special shops. There was not much difference in the wages paid to those who made garments for the stores and those who made custom work, except that the latter received better prices for higher class goods in costly suits.

Clothes did not then cost the working man much more than they do now, for a very good suit of satinet, which cost but little more than at the present time, would do for two or three years as a Sunday suit, and then overalls were more generally worn on work days. The ordinary business suits, and the cheaper grade of goods are much cheaper today, because labor is very much cheaper. A coat is now made in the New York shops for sixty-two and one-half cents which would formerly cost three or four dollars. A whole suit may be made now for ninety-nine cents which formerly would bring the tailor seven or eight dollars.

The sewing machine, one of the greatest of modern economic inventions, has been introduced into this industry and has revolutionized the business. There are, at least, 30,000 garment makers in New York City, and these will make, at a very low estimate, 30,000,000 suits in a year. There may be 20,000 more engaged in the same business in other cities, and these annually make 20,000,000 more suits, making 50,000,000 in all—sufficient to clothe the entire male population of the land. There are about 50,000 engaged in custom tailoring in the United States, and with the sewing machine to facilitate work in this branch of the industry also, it is evident that the markets must be well supplied with clothing.

In 1860 there were 91,670 men and women employed in making clothing, and their wages amounted to $15,996,009, about $175 for each person. In 1890 this number had increased to about 140,000 employees, and the average wages was about $385 a year for each worker. This would seem to indicate an increase of more than double the amount of wages, but the same ratio of increase in the number of employees was not verified. Statistics, however, in regard to wages in this industry are not very reliable. The task system of a day's work prevails in a great majority of these shops, and good wages may be paid for a nominal day's work, but the number of garments the operator is compelled to finish for a day's wages requires two and even two and one-half days of persistent labor to accomplish. The wages then may be two dollars a day, but the toilers are only able to put in two and two-fifth days a week, and this cuts their pay down to $4.80 a week.   The actual wages earned by these workers in May, 1897, are: Tailors from $3 to $5 a week; children's jacket makers about $2 a week; trousers makers about $3 a week; knee pants makers $5 a week; vest makers $4 a week.* The census figures seem to indicate prosperity and advance of wages; but, unfortunately, they are unreliable and untrue.

Twenty years ago the garment makers of New York, who now toil long hours for $4 and $5 a week, could make $25 a week; yet, with the help of   the   blessed   machine   and   with   modern

*New York World, May 20, 1897.

methods, their producing power is now fully as much as it was then.

The census of 1860 says of the sewing machine: "The application of its use in the last ten years has been revolutionary. It has opened avenues to profitable and healthful industry for thousands of industrious females to whom the labor of the needle had become wholly unremunerative and injurious in their effects. Like all automatic powers it has enhanced the comforts of every class by cheapening the process of manufacture without permanently substracting from the average means of support of any portion of the community."

In the light of later developments the above extract would seem to have been intended for humorous irony were it not printed in such a solemn work as a compilation of census facts and figures. The half starved forms, and the sickly features of the garment makers tell more strongly than ironical guess-work how profitable and healthful is this industry!

It seems to be an admitted principle in political economy that cheapening the process of manufacture adds to the sum of human comforts and consequent human happiness. When the cheapening process is effected by lowering the rate of wages, or by displacing hand labor, then the product, in theory, is placed within the reach of the greater number; but in practice this method reduces the consuming power of the laboring class, which is the most numerous, and decreases their means of enjoying these comforts. If this displacement of labor or lowering the rates of wages, in the cheapening process of manufacture, took place in one industry alone cheap products might be a blessing; but when all industries are similarly affected the cheap comforts are placed within the reach of the few, whilst the general effect is a decrease of the consuming power of the working class and a great addition to the sum of human misery.

The law of supply and demand must regulate the rate of wages. The introduction of the sewing machine has lessened the demand for labor, and must, inevitably, lower the rate of wages.

The wages paid to the garment makers have been gradually descending the scale until at the present time they have reached the starvation mark. Overproduction and greed are the causes of this decline. The retail clothier in his desire for trade and large profit, demands a cheaper garment from the wholesaler, so that he may undersell his competitor and increase his sales. The manufacturer wishes to preserve his share of the profits, and, consequently, he pays less to the contractor for having the garments made. The contractor seeks the cheapest labor in the market so that he may have the largest possible profit, and as the supply of this kind of labor exceeds the demand large numbers may be found ready to work for any wages that will keep the wolf from their door.

To save rent contractors had the garments made in tenement houses, or in "sweat shops," where the workers were huddled together like cattle. Anxiety to sell their goods made smaller and less reputable houses resort to all means of cheap production so they could undersell their competitors; and the garment makers had in all cases to suffer when the selling price was reduced. Suits now retailing at $5 and $6 formerly sold for $10 and $12, though the material is the same. The difference in price represents the toiler's loss.

Small manufacturers in New York could make up garments cheaper than the large houses, because they had little shops in a poor part of the city, and they could do their own designing and cutting; or they turned their living rooms into shops, thus saving the expense of rent. The larger houses are obliged to sell their goods in the same markets, and to meet the cut of the small dealers they pay less to the contractors, and these in turn reduce the wages of the tailors. This process could not be completed if the producing power did not far exceed the consumption. But what can the poor tailors do when every other trade is in the same condition? The duller the clothing business is the more does the "sweat shop" thrive, for then the dealers strive to stimulate trade by lowering the cost of production.

We can scarcely conceive how those poor creatures can live and support families on $4 or $5 a week. Some of them do not live, they starve to death. Mrs. Becker of Brooklyn died of starvation, March 20, 1896, because her poor tailor husband could not earn money enough to buy nourishing food for her body. He made $3.50 when he worked a full week, and yet our political economy friend, and the statistical fiends tell us that wages are higher now than they ever were in the past, and the cost of living is less now than it has been for generations. Other wise men tell us that drink is the cause of poverty, and the wretched condition of the tailors. But where can these poor beings find time to drink when they work sixteen or eighteen hours a day? Drink costs money; and how can these poor slaves spare a few pennies from their poverty wages to spend in luxury?

The "sweat shop" is the natural outgrowth of the contract system. The large manufacturers agree with the contractors* upon a certain price for the making of suits and garments out of

*The reduction in prices paid to contractors amounts to fully 50 per cent in recent years.

cloth already cut, and these contractors hire the cheapest labor they can find in the market, and strive for the greatest amount of production at the least possible cost. Tailors living in cheap, poorly ventilated tenements, and who make work shops out of their living rooms, or who huddle together in cheaply rented rooms, can afford to work for less than those who labor under more favorable conditions. About 70 per cent. of the garment makers of New York are laboring in the "sweat shops," or in unhealthful living rooms, so that they may underbid competitors for the work at wages which will keep them from starving.

Twenty years ago most of the work in the making of garments was done by hand, and a long apprenticeship was necessary before one could be classed as a skilled worker. Now nearly all the work is done by machines, except the basting, the pressing and the finishing. At first the machine was used for sewing the sleeves of the coat, and its use was gradually extended until at present it is used for all the sewing done in the making of the coat and other garments, with the exception of the button holes.

There is now a machine for making the button holes, and its work cannot be distinguished from the hand work of the tailor, especially when it is touched up by a skillful finisher. One machine can do the work of at least six men, and when we consider that there are about 100,000 garment workers in the United States, of whom, perhaps, 20,000 are operators, we can estimate what an enormous displacement of labor has taken place in this one branch of industry. The machine for making button holes displaces a greater proportion of labor than does the ordinary sewing machine, and 150,000 is a conservative estimate of the number of toilers in this branch of industry who have been displaced by the introduction of labor-saving machinery. Some writers on industrial questions assert that the sewing machine has displaced no one, but has been a great labor-saving blessing to humanity. Writers of this school claim also that if any workers are accidentally displaced by machines they may find employment in the new industries created by the expansion of labor in supplying new machinery to meet the changed conditions. These writers, howeer, seem to overlook the primary principle of economic development, in the institution of machinery for hand work, which is to lower the cost of production. If the men displaced by machinery, in the actual work of producing, could find employment in the new industry created by the demand for the machinery which has displaced them, their wages would not be saved to the producers but must be still added to the cost of production, and thus the introduction of labor-saving machinery would defeat its own purpose.

In 1890 there were about 9,000 persons engaged in the sewing machine making industry; and we have seen that these 9,000 represent the number that could find employment in the new industry out of 100,000 displaced in the garment making trades.

It would be very difficult to gather statistics which would show the displacement of labor which has taken place in other departments of the needle industry through the introduction of

the sewing machine.   In the making of ladies'
clothes, in the making of household and decora-
tive goods, the displacement has been enormous.
The displacement which has taken place in these
departments far exceeds the displacement of
labor in the male garment making trades; and
hundreds of thousands of women and girls, who
are now working for $3 or $4 a week in stores,
or who are crowding men out of their own field,
or who are idle, could find profitable and appro-
priate employment at needle work, if the labor-
saving machine had never been placed upon the
market.

There are thousands of girls in Greater New
York,* young and intelligent, willing to work,
but they cannot find any work to do.   Needle
work should open a very promising field to the
cunning hand and the quick eye of youth, and
should give profitable employment to hundreds
of thousands of females who are profitably fitted
for the light, quick movements of needle-work.

The whirr of the machines are heard in the
shops instead of the light cheery voices of youth,

*Fourteenth Annual Report Labor Bureau, N.Y.

and bread is taken from the mouths of thousands that economic inventions may be applied to the producing trades. Love for mankind has no place here; this is business, and machines are more profitable than human hands. Gold is God; and girls may starve or go on the streets.*

The sewing machine might be a blessing to mankind if it were used to lessen the burden of labor, but like all labor-saving machines it is employed to reduce the cost of production, and consequently to crush the laborer and to enrich the capitalist. Men do not intend directly to injure their fellow men; but sentiment has no place in business, and nothing can interefere with money making except the strong power of prohibitive law.

We have already seen how the sewing machine has been adapted to the boot and shoe industry, and the number of toilers it has displaced

*Many of the young girls arrested in New York as street walkers, are factory girls and clerks who cannot make a living at their work. Many young married women are arrested for the same reason, because their husbands are obliged to work for starvation wages. (Interview with Police Captain Chapman of New York.)

in this and the clothing trades; yet there are experts* who assert that this invention has not displaced any one. It would seem as if the whole theory of economics had gone wrong when such an idiotic conclusion can pass for scientific lore. No one labor-saving invention has been so generally applied or has displaced so many women and men in the manufacturing industries as the sewing machine. Instead of being a blessing to humanity it has been a curse, and instead of relieving the worker of the heavy burden of toil it has only added to his misery; has lengthened his hours of labor; has reduced his wages until he has become a slave that he may live; or has turned him into a kind of associate machine that needs food and repose much as the sewing machine requires oil and repairs.

The cotton mills of Maine and Massachusetts have flooded the markets with the enormous products of their labor saving methods of manufacture, and the owners have forced the operatives into strikes so that they can restrict production until the markets recuperate. The new

*Commissioner of Labor, Carroll D. Wright.

cotton mills of the South have also entered the field, and with the latest labor-saving devices, cheap child labor, and enjoying local economic advantages over their older rivals in New England, have brought a stagnation in the industry through overproduction.

The New England manufacturers resort to the old expedient of cutting wages to meet the superior advantages of the mills of the South. Wages are already below the "living wage," but what can the poor operatives do, but strike and starve. Are the great mass of toilers to gaze idly on, and see this crazy economic principle ruin the land?

The manufacturers are urging the government to aid them in securing foreign markets for their goods, by new steamship lines, by subsidies, through the consular agencies, and by greater facilities of obtaining patents on labor-saving methods of manufacture, whilst they are reducing the wages of their employees. What right have they to make the government an accomplice in their unconscious conspiracy to bring disaster upon the land? Does the government

exist merely for the benefit of a few manufacturers?   Have the great mass of toilers no
rights?   They have; but they lack concentrated
intelligence and strength to enforce them.

CHAPTER IV.

The ancient and honorable trade of house-making is as old as the world. No sooner were men in the world than they sought a sheltering place to protect them from the heat and the cold, from sunshine and from storm. The first shelters were necessarily rude rough strongholds, built for protection more than for comfort, and beauty of design and grandeur of construction did not form any feature of the buildings until men had attained ease and comparative wealth.

The ready made materials which nature supplied in abundance, formed the little structure for shelter, and an embryo home. Men may have first constructed rude huts, like the wig-wams of the Algonquins, but with the advent of civilization and the spread of the knowledge of the mechanic arts arose the great lumber business and the house building trades. The vast forests in every part of the world offered materials that only needed the skill of man to fashion them into forms of beauty and graceful outline, that not only served as a shelter but also as an attractive ornament to the dwelling of man.

Felling the trees in the vast forests, cutting them into logs, bringing them to the mills, where they are sawed into boards of a suitable length and thickness to serve the carpenter's use, have always formed a great industry, employing thousands of expert and skilled men in the different branches of the trade. The old fashioned axe in the hands of the chopper is the usual method of felling trees in the United States. The industrial revolution, however, has invaded this field as it has every other and steam power has been applied in the large lumber camps, where the conditions are favorable, to the felling of trees. When the genius of man shall have perfected means of applying electricity and compressed air to small motor engines, who can say how far machine power will supercede the hand work of man?

As the sculptor chisels the marble into most graceful and majestic forms of beauty so does the skilled artist in wood carve it into most intricate and delicate lines of tracery or into massive

forms of architectural ornament. All the graceful lines and forms of beauty in the cornices,
frieze, capital and column of the encircling
models of the Gothic, Doric, Tuscan, Ionic,
Corinthian, Moorish, or the more modern styles of
architecture, are the handiwork of men, with the
simple tools that are entirely operated by hand.
There is scarecely any limit to the degree of skill
that can be attained and the amount of work
that can be accomplished in shaping wood to the
different purposes of architecture to office or domestic use, and as cunning as the hand may
become in the use of tools modern labor-saving
machinery will follow close in its wake, turning
out shaopely ornaments with astonishing rapidity.

Machines are made to supplant the sculptor's
art, and, with a goood hand-made model as an ex-
amplar, busts or medallions of noted individuals
may be turned off in an hour that would require
sixty hours of labor by hand. It is true that to
satisfy artistic taste the finishing touches must
be done by hand to the finer grade of machine
carving; but for all rough work which will only

be viewed at a distance, such as ornaments for ships and lofty buildings, the machine finish is all sufficient. Works that do not follow regular or geometric curves in their outlines, such as the gunstock, may be carved rapidly and thoroughly by revolving machinery.

Machinery has been introduced into the manufacture of all the ornamental grades of household furniture, and the parts of a chair, a desk, or a bedstead, are quickly turned into pleasing forms in grace and outline by the rapid revolving machine. Machine work is apt to be flimsy, and much of the machine-made furniture is merely a veneer of carving whilst the solid and more costly ornamentation is the work of hand.

We can undersell European makers in the cheaper grades of furniture, because our superior machinery enables us to manufacture at less cost. In most European countries the homes of the wealthier class are adorned with fine old massive furniture, carved by hand. Germany especially is very well supplied with very high class art furniture, but offers a good market for our factory products of the cheaper grades.*

Twenty-five or thirty years ago all the doors, sashes, blinds and frames used in the construction of a house were made by hand. Then the carpenter's trade was an honorable avocation, which required not only skill but also a long course of apprenticeship to perfect the tyro in all the mysteries of the calling. Now the planing mills turn out doors, and sashes, and blinds, and frames of every description in vast quantities, and any man who is handy with the hammer, the saw and the screw-driver, may put them together.

Before planing mills invaded the field of skilled labor, carpenters could find profitable work during the whole year. In the winter season they could plane, and hew, and cut and carve the doors, the jambs, the sashes, the blinds and all the ornamental work for a building in their comfortable shops, and when the pleasant spring season came again they were prepared for

*E. S. W. Taylor, United States Consul at Brunswick.

the outdoor work, which was generally abundant and profitable. Now carpenters are idle in the winter season, except occasionally some half starved tradesmen are found, shivering in the cold at some job, for a pittance to keep the wolf from the door. All the preparatory work is done by the planing mills; and one skilled hand, with a few handy laborers can do all the joining and fitting of the parts made in the factory.

And this is progress, this is machine civilization!

In 1850 the census returns gave 184,671 as the number of carpenters in the United States; in 1880 there were only 54,138 reported as engaged in this occupation, whilst in the census of 1890 the number 140,021 was returned as the total following this calling. The population of the United States had about trebled itself in the period from 1850 to 1890; building operations and carpenter work, in repairing, car building and many other forms of woodwork, increased in volume fully as fast as the population increased in numbers, and we should find in 1890 half a million men employed in the carpenter's trade. Instead of the half million of skilled citizens following this extensive trade, we find but a little more than one-eighth of a million of poor paid, half starved mechanics, who can not find work through six months of the year. And this is the new civilization!

There are men who imagine that this displacement of labor by machinery is a benefit to the industrial world, that it is a sign of the progress of the age. Whom does it benefit? Not the skilled tradesman; for his skill no longer commands high wages, and he must struggle to get employment for a few months in the year. Planing mill owners and builders may have made fortunes out of the changed conditions, in the early stages of the machine era, but competition has cut down their profits in recent years and they are now in a worse condition than they were under the old system of hand work. Planing mills, that do the preparatory carpenter work, have sprung up in every place where there was a prospect of extensive building until they could no longer find sale for their products, and failures followed.

There is no prospect of a return to old and prosperous methods. Some even imagine that prosperity can be brought back by still further extending the present insane labor displacing methods. The wood working machinery manufacturers have organized a trust, whose purpose, they declare, is to decrease the cost of manufacture.* They have lessened the cost of production in the past by displacing labor; and this seems to be the principal, and about the only idea inventors have of decreasing the cost of manufacture. These geniuses do not seem to realize that they are laboring in a vicious circle, that they defeat their own purpose. Their object is to increase the amount of production, and at the same time to lessen the cost; but they directly cripple the consuming power by their methods, and production without consumption is necessarily a loss .

Years ago upholstering was an important trade, which gave employment to thousands of men at good wages. Taste and skill were necessary for the artisan, and the wages paid were

*New York, December 18, 1897.

about the highest in any of the trades. Labor-
saving inventions invaded this industry, broke
up the little shops, and sent adrift thousands of
skilled workmen who were obliged to seek other
occupations or join the great army of the unemployed.*

*The New York papers, Feb. 8, 1898, report the
case of Joseph Schmeder who is a skilled uphol-
sterer, and who kept an establishment in New
York years ago that employed many men. Labor-
saving machines forced him out of business. He
managed to get along for a time with a few jobs,
because he was a skilled workman, but he kept running behind until he finally succumbed to starvation.

CHAPTER V.

PRISON LABOR.

The State Legislatures have adopted various methods of utilizing the time of the convicts committed to their penal institutions. In New York State, under the law which went into effect January 1, 1897, convicts are employed under State management in the manufacture of goods and articles which may be sold to any other institutions of the State or to any division of the State, that is, to any branch of town or municipal government. Prison labor is not allowed to compete in open market with free labor, but it has an exclusive market of its own; as all the institutions of the State and all the branches of town and municipal government are obliged to buy whatever manufactured articles they use from the penal institutions.*

The workingmen of the State are taxed for the support of these penal institutions, and it is rank injustice to them to be excluded from a

*This is the construction that has been put on this law.

market for their products through favor to an element which has no standing in law. If our penal institutions must engage in manufactures, on the plea of keeping the inmates occupied, there is no reason whatsoever why they should be allowed to employ labor-saving machinery.* The advocates of labor-saving machinery claim that their use is a symbol of civilization and progress, because they take the burden of toil from the hand of man and render more facile and rapid the process of manufacture. Convicts are condemned to hard labor, and it is not sympathy that inspires interested parties to alleviate their lot. It looks very much as if the desire of placing money, the earnings of convicts, in the hands of officials were the inspiration of the Legislature.

There is an ample field of employment for prison labor in improving the highways of the State without coming in competition with any kind of free labor. Every State in the Union could be vastly improved by better roads. The bicycle has been so generally adopted by all

**No machinery can be used in Massachusetts except such as is propelled by hana or foot power. Stimson.

classes that it has become the ordinary means of transportation for vast numbers of people in country as well as town. The country roads are not in any state in such condition that wheeling may be found comfortable or even practicable. The State makes enormous appropriations for the improvement of canals and waterways, in the interests of commerce; it fosters the railways to facilitate transportation of goods, and why not improve the roadways of the land to promote wheeling for business or for pleasure?

No public improvement could promote the interests of any state in a greater measure than the construction of good roads, and no outlay would show better results in the pleasure of bicyclists and the profit of the farmer. The automobile is yet in its infancy, is a mere pretty toy, but it has power, endurance, speed and cheapness, and it may yet be put to practical use in the transportation of goods and products. Good roads are a necessity for the introduction of this latest fin de siecle wonder, and it would be for the interests of the State to have the roads in such condition that this invention may be used with pleasure and profit. It would bring the markets to the farmer's door, and with the abolishment by law of the bonanza farms of the South and West—those ravenous monsters that devour the food markets of the world—plenty and prosperity may again bring joy and comfort to the farmer's home.

All the convicts of the State could be employed to advantage in the construction of roads, under the supervision of competent engineers; and they would only displace the farmers in this work who now make the roads impassable at certain seasons by the use of the most convenient but improper material.

The State should not be a competitor in the market with free labor, nor should it enter a field of industry which is amply covered by private enterprise.

Some states allow their convicts to be leased to contractors for work outside the prison walls.* Other states only allow their convicts to be em-

*Indiana, Michigan, Nebraska, West Virginia, Kentucky, Tennessee, Arkansas, Texas, Nevada, South Carolina, Alabama, Mississippi, Florida, New Mexico, Arizona, "Handbook to the Labor Law of United States," Stimson.

ployed outside the prison walls on works under iec direct control of the state;* others only permit contract work within prison walls;** whilst other states restrict the work to certain goods not manufactured elsewhere in the state.***

Criminals should everywhere be withdrawn from the competition with free labor, and the State should leave the labor market free to its citizens. If our legislators wished to add to the criminal population of the State, they could have taken no more insidious and effective measures to accomplish this end than by taking away from the toilers some of the necessary means of earning a livelihood. There is not work enough now in the State for all its citizen toilers, and the opportunities of employment have been lessened by the introduction of the convict element. They may say that prison labor does not compete with free labor in the open market, because it is only the case is even worse than open competition would be, because the products of free labor are allowed to supply goods to State institutions. But

*Ida. Const., Ibid.
**Minnesota, Wisconsin, Kansas, Missouri, Ibid.
***Maine, Colorado, Ibid.

absolutely excluded from this portion of the market, and prison labor has a practical monopoly.

Some say this system of prison labor is favorable to the taxpayers of the State. This is a fake, pure and simple. Prison goods are not sold to state or municipal institutions at a lower price than these institutions would have to pay for the same goods to citizen dealers. The Fire Commissioners of Buffalo state that nine dozen of horse brushes, ordered from Auburn prison, cost them $27 more than the same would cost them if purchased in open market. One commissioner said: "That is a damnable law at the best and a gross outrage. It could be termed robbery without overstepping the bounds of reason."* Another commisisoner said: "This law leaves us helpless to protect our interests and the rights of the taxpayers."**

The object of this law is evidently to give political rings the handling of State money. It is another step in the enslavement of the masses.

*W. S. Grattan.
**John F. Malone.

The great body of free toilers of the State are
base caitiffs if they do not teach these political
fakirs* a lesson in American citizenship.

No power driven machinery is used in the
manufacture of articles of commerce in the
Western Penitentiary of Pennsylvania, and
workingmen should see that the same wise pro-
vision should prevail in every penal institution
in the land. It seems incomprehensible that
labor leaders should recommend the recently introduced New York State system as a model to
the other states. This system has not even the excuse of economy for its existence. It is more
injurious to labor than direct competition, because it practically excludes labor from a large
and profitable market. There are many ways
of employing convicts at hard labor without in-
flicting an injury upon the upright part of the
community.

Public sentiment might not approve of the
old fashioned chain gangs of convicts being
made a spectacle on the highways, but surely
there is inventive genius enough in this age to

*Political rings defeated the anti-trust laws.

obviate this difficulty. The Governor of Massachusetts and the General Superintendent of Prisons there have just recommended the employment of convicts of their state in the construction of a canal. An enclosure is to be built around the place of employment, to screen the convicts from public gaze and to prevent escape. Such an enclosure could be made movable. If this scheme works well in the construction of a canal, it should be adapted to the building of a highway.

CHAPTER VI.

INVENTIONS.

The nineteenth century has been the most remarkable in the history of the world for the
number and importance of practical inventions,
and the application of the latent powers of nature to the uses of man.

In looking backward now over the past one
hundred years of development it seems scarcely
credible that so many inventions, absolutely
necessary to progress under present conditions,
could have been so long hidden from man, and
that the powers of nature, which have existed
from the beginning of the world, should have
lain dormant through so many generations.
"Why should the spirit of man be proud!"
There are yet undoubtedly undiscovered and un-
developed powers in the great storehouse of
nature, which would eclipse the remarkable dis-
coveries of the present century.

At the beginning of the present century very
little was known of the nature and the power
of steam, of the possibility of its use as a sub-

stitute for horse power in transportation, or for water power in the propulsion of machinery. Steam was first used for propelling vessels in 1802, and we can easily understand what a revolution this has wrought in the maritime commerce of the world. The great Atlantic liners now cross the ocean in six or seven days, carrying thousands of tons of freight, and a moderate sized village on their passenger list. With favoring winds twenty-one days was a very quick passage by sail from Liverpool to New York; and, considering the facilities for loading and unloading, a modern first-class steamer could make three or four trips to the sturdy old lumbering sailing vessel's one. Four or five times the number of sailing vessels would be required to do the business that is now done by the steam merchant marine of the world. We can behold in imagination the congested condition of the East River and the North River in New York with four or five times the present number of vessels there, seeking dockage to load and unload their passengers and freight. We can imagine what an immense fleet of sailing vessels would crowd around the great Liverpool docks under old conditions to transact the business that is now done there by the swift ocean steamers. Every sea and lake port in the world would require three or four times the present number of vessels if steamers were displaced by sailing craft to transact their present amount of business. To the eyes of most people great fleets of vessels, with their forests of masts, are indications of commercial energy and prosperity, and with sailing vessels alone to traverse the seas and lakes new life would be infused into many a dead old town. The world would not be willing to return to the former slow method. The old style would indeed give employment to many thousands more, but considerations of humanity do not enter into the calculations of progress in this age.

To save time, and to save money in transportation, as wel las in production, without regard to incidental results or disastrous effects upon the toilers, has been the tendency of economic progress, and has been the chief aim of the teaching of modern political economy. The toilers, as a whole, have reaped no benefits from improved methods, notwithstanding what the census sharps may say. The whole advance has been made in the line of economic production and transportation.

Steam power has been utilized in agriculture, displacing hand labor and horse power to a very large extent. The steam thresher has been a familiar sight for many years on country roads, and in a few days it does the work that would require the work of two or three men during a whole winter to complete. Plowing, too, is now done by steam on the large farms of the South and West. The greatest labor-saving mammoth of all devices for farm work has been put in operation in California. This does the work of the mower, the reaper, the binder, and the thresher, all at the same time, and also puts the grain into sacks ready for the market, by the same operation. It is operated by steam and cuts a swath line fifty-two feet wide; so it is cap-able of an immense amount of work.

The use of steam as a motor power wrought a revolution in the transportation business of the world. Railroads were unknown previous to 1804; passengers and freight were carried across country in the heavy wagons drawn by horses or oxen; on the canals in boats drawn by horses; and on large bodies of water by the slow going sailing craft. It would require three or four months by the old method to transport grain from the wheat fields of the West to the markets of Europe, and about one hundred per cent. would be added to the cost. Two weeks now would be sufficient time for transporting grain that distance, and the cost is not one-tenth what it would be under the old system.

The steam snow plow on the railways has displaced an immense amount of hand labor. Traffic on the railways, after a heavy fall of snow, used to be a very serious problem before the invention of the steam snow plow; snow drifts would either stop traffic or would necessitate the employment of hundreds of hands; now the combined power of several engines drives the great plow through heavy drifts of snow with almost irresistible force. The signal and the block system on railways, and in fact, all the railroad improve-

ments are inventions of the present century.
Switches are manipulated by levers, in a group,
at a distance, to save the labor of men at the different tracks.

In the manner of handling grain, in the loading and unloading of cars and vessels, a most
wonderful improvement has been made. The
handling of millions of bushels of grain, in the
rail, lake and sea transportation would be a
serious problem under the old system and would
involve the employment of a vast army of men.
The great elevators run a long leg like the
snout of a mammoth into the hold of a
vessel and suck up the grain with the power and
rapidity of a typhoon sucking up the sand in the
desert, whilst another automatic conductor con-
veys the grain to the storage lines, to canal boats
or to the railroad cars for overland transportation. Great shovels, operated by machinery,
have displaced, in a measure, the scoopers in
feeding grain to the leg that so rapidly unloads
the vessels.

Powerful and rapid moving weaving machines
have displaced the hand looms; and immense

spinning jacks have forced out the slow going solitary wheel, which is no longer seen except in histrionic representations of medieval simplicity. These two inventions alone have increased in a most wonderful manner the products of manufacture. In 1770 the amount of manufactured cotton produced in England was about two and one-half million pounds; and experts claimed that this amount could not be increased one hundred per cent. in thirty years, even though all available workers were taught the secrets of the trade and employed in the business. Inventions, however, were shortly afterwards placed upon the market that upset all these calculations, and at the beginning of the new century British manufacturers were placing upon the market a yearly product of thirty-seven million pounds, with an increase in a quarter of a century of about one hundred per cent. of operators and an increase of over fifteen hundred per cent. of products.* Operatives in these branches at the present time cannot find continued imployment,

*Mallock. "The Labor Problem and the Public Welfare."

though their numbers are greatly reduced; and they are compelled to be idle a portion of the year, or work for small wages.

There is scarcely a branch of industry in which manual labor is extensively employed that has not been invaded by the ubiquitous Yankee inventive genius, to learn how he may substitute some patent mechanical device for hand work. Imitation is the underlying principle in all these inventions. Every movement of the hand may be duplicated by machinery, and all the wonderful skill and cunning that have been acquired by hands through years of practice in the fine and different branches of manufacture are imitated by complex movements of machinery. The delicate works of a watch are made by machinery and they only need the hand of man to combine them and to place them in position. Intricate work in wood carving is done by machines, and lines that do not follow regular curves or geometric figure, such as gunstocks, may be traced by these man-supplanting devices.

Where great power is necessary vast machines worked by steam have superceded the hand work of men. Dredging machines hoist more earth from the water in five minutes than could be raised by a dozen men in as many hours. The ponderous trip hammers, with their appliances, beat into desired shape immense shafts of iron and steel that could not be handled by hand implements, or that would require a small army of men to handle and to hammer into the proper form.

Machinery has in a great measure displaced men in the building of railroads and canals. It is stated* that the machinery sent to the Isthmus of Panama would do the work of one-half million of men. The work of building the Erie canal was a gigantic task and gave employment to ten thousand men for seven or eight years, but in those days only the pick, the shovel and the wheelbarrow were used. With the same implements the Isthmus of Panama would have given employment to many thousands more for a much longer period.

The most notable inventions in labor-saving machinery in the present century are manifest

*"Recent Economic Changes." Wells.

in the art of printing. From the discovery of the
art up to the beginning of the present century
no perceptible improvement had been made.
Generation after generation of printers stood
alongside their cases and set their type in the
good old fashioned style. The press was usually
worked by hand, and even as late as 1825 hand
presses alone were found in many of the large
metropolitan printing offices.

Horse power constituted the first step in improvement over the hand press. The horse
power method seeems laughable enough now,
with our innumerable steam and electric motors,
but at its first introduction it was an evidence of
enterprise and progress. The horse was usually
placed in the cellar or a room beneath the press,
and there by moving in a circle, much after the
manner of moving buildings now, he furnished
the rotary motion for the great printing establishments.

Up to the second decade of the present century the presses were mere wooden affairs, with
vice and lever attachments for making impres-
sions with each successive movement. In 1820

Lord Stanhope perfected a machine in which the bar was not directly attached to the vice but to an outside cylinder by which a counter weight brought back the platen at each blow. Soon afterwards other improvements were made until the introduction of steam when the whole business was revolutionized.

The great newspaper printing machines of the present day are vast, complicated, automata, that do the work of scores of skillful hands.* They unroll and cut the paper; they print and fold the newspaper, and they count the number of copies that leave the press. When colored supplements are used a latteral department of these mammoths will stamp the sheets with the proper figures and colors, and will regularly place each one in its proper place in the main copy as this enters the folding department. Man is merely necessary to write the news and to keep the machine oiled, and who knows what wonderful changes may not be made in these departments in the coming years!

*"Seventy-five men with the labor-saving printing inventions can do the same amount of work that formerly would require ten thousand men." Moody.

The process of displacing labor has been going on in trades allied to printing, and in the making of type and paper machines have superceding hand work. In the early part of the century old fashioned moulds were in use for making type; then distinct type foundries began to spring up, and intricate machinery took the place of hand labor. The latest and highest development of type making as well as type setting is found in the linotype, in which the type is instantly moulded as required for use by a simple touch of the finger upon a key, as in the typewriter, and the lettered type is formed and drops into place ready for the impression. After use this type is thrown into the molten metel in the heated tank, where it is dissolved and forms part of the liquid lead which only awaits the opening of the key touched by the finger of the skilled operator to drop into the mould and form a letter ready for the press. This process is capable of still further development, and it is within the range of possibilities for an operator at New York, or some other news center, to set up the type on these machines by electricity for all the newspapers in the State. Men are no longer necessary except to furnish the brain power, touch a button and electricity will do the rest.

Most wonderful changes have taken place in all the metal working trades, and machines have forced all the hand implements and nearly all the skilled mechanics out of the business. The skill of the trained mechanic is only required for the highest grade of work, or to put the finishing touches on the machine products. Firearms, which were formerly made by hand are now made almost entirely by machines. One man now with machinery can do fifty times the amount of work formerly done by hand.

Twenty-five or thirty years ago carriage making was a respectable and profitable trade that gave employment to skilled citizens in every village and town in the country; and in the large cities thousands found steady work and good wages in making the finer grade of carriages, in difficult wheelwright work, or in the allied trades of blacksmithing and carriage painting, which were carried on in the same shop. Factories have now obliterated the small shops; machines have displaced skilled men, and a few hundred medium priced handy men do the work that should give employment to thousands of skilled citizens at high wages.

What distinct gain can be discovered for civilization or for humanity in this change? Thousands of wagons, sleighs, buggies and carriages of every description, of an inferior grade, have been placed on the market because the manufacturers were allured with the prospect of greater profit on account of cheaper methods of production, whilst thousands of skilled artizans have been forced out of this well paying trade to seek a livelihood in some other branch of industry. If this is what our pseudo political economists call progress and the signs of advancing civilization, then the ordinary eye is not fitted to see things in the rarified atmosphere of this higher science. The enormous profits promised by cheaper production did not fulfill expectations. Greed, as usual, led makers to overstock the market, and then competition reduced prices, and the fabulous fortunes of sweet anticipation vanished like the mists.

Vessel building was formerly a great industry, giving employment to thousands upon thousands of skilled mechanics at good wages. The ship carpenter was envied by the house carpenter, because he had steady work and good wages and he always knew the locality of his daily labor. Machinery has displaced labor at an enormous rate in the ship building trades. It is true that iron and steel enters largely now into the construction of vessels, but machinery also has taken the place of men, and now one man with the aid of machinery can do the same amount of work that four or five men could formerly do by hand.* Band saws cut large timbers into the desired shape, in one half hour, that would require the labor of ten men a half day to hew and plane and chisel to proper form. The hand calker is no longer needed; the work is now done by machinery. Drilling holes for bolts or rivets is done by machinery.

In 1850 there were 14,585 ship carpenters, 1,915 caulkers, and the blacksmiths must have been able to present an imposing number; and

*Report of the Commissioner of Labor, 1886.

yet the country at that time did not do one-
tenth of the amount of commerce which it did
forty years later, but in 1890 there were only
25,934 altogether reported as engaged in ship
building.*   If the number of persons employed
in this business had increased in the same ratio
as the commerce of the country there should be
at least 200,000 reported for this industry in
1890.

In 1850 the census reported 99,703 blacksmiths; in 1880 the number was 50,634, and in
this number was included wheelwrights, and in
1890 the number of these two classes was 50,-
867.**   If we compute the prosperity of the
country by the volume of trade, the country is
progressing finely; if we compute prosperity by
the relative number employed, it is going backward.

In the manufacture of wine machinery has
been introduced to take the place of hand labor.
A crushing machine with one man will easily do

*Census, 1890.
**Our Census officials have mixed up the trades
in such a manner that it is difficult to institute ex-
act comparisons.

the same amount of work in a day that was formerly done by eight men with hand machines. Even the hand crushers are machine methods in comparison with the hand, or rather foot, system of crushing grapes, much in vogue in some parts of Europe. The wine is not improved by machine methods; it even deteriorates, because the machines crush the seeds and add the acid, bitter flavor of the seeds to the mature nature sweetened juice of the grapes. But this is progress!

Machines do the fine and difficult work of planing, turning and shaping the wood work for musical instruments, and one boy with the aid of a machine can do the work of twenty-five men.

One man with modern machinery can turn out about two hundred and seventy-eight sounding boards in a day, whilst formerly four was a good day's work for an expert artisan.*

Cigar making was, until labor-saving devices were introduced into the business, one of the great trades, giving employment to thousands of men at good wages. Cigarette making offered

*Report of the Commissioner of Labor, 1886.

remunerative employment to thousands of girls, because here neatness and dexterity were of more importance than expert skill. The machine has now driven man and girl from these occupations except in some of the smaller shops where they still cling to hand methods, or in the finer grades of work, because inventive genius has not yet been able to give to machines the cunning of the hand of man. A great trust has been formed of the cigarette factories, and the old hand methods that gave employment to hundreds and thousands have been abolished, and machines have been substituted for girls; they do more work and they lessen the cost of production. This is the result of enlightened economy and fin de siecle civilization. One girl with a modern machine can make more cigarettes in a day than ten girls could make by hand. Machines for making cigars displace, at least, three times the number of men that would be required without their use.

Machines are used for turning out pills by the thousand; machines make pins and needles, and they make the fine and intricate parts of clocks and watches.

In Switzerland there are forty thousand persons employed in watch making. If the labor-saving machinery used in the same industry in the United States were introduced there only eight thousand four hundred would be required to turn out the same amount of work. Their statesmen may not believe in the crazy quilt philosophy that guides our theorists here, and they may not put into practice the pauperizing principles of political economy that lead to industrial depression and starvation.

The wonderful powers of electricity have been applied of late years to the principles of production, not only in supplying motor power but also in the working of metals where heat is required for solution or combination. Man has not yet learned to utilize to its fullest extent all the subtle capabilities of this magic power. How much of an aid will it be to man in assisting him to extract food and wealth from the great storehouse of nature? In what measure will it displace man in the actual field of labor? It al-

ready goes down into the mine and helps to extract the ore; it furnishes the motor power to
haul the ore to the smelting works or the re-
fining factory; it supplies heat for smelting,
moulding and amalgamating metals; it has revolutionized the methods of lighting cities and of
transporting passengers, and yet men have only
mastered the rudimentary principles of its application.

Electricity has displaced labor in some works,
but figures are not available to show the amount
of such displacement. It is related that the
most wonderful change Mr. Carnegie noted
during his three years' absence from one of his
works, was effected by the substitution of electricity for hand work; three men with the aid of
machines and electricity could do the same
amount of work that three hundred men could
formerly do by old methods. The practical application is in its infancy yet. It can be made
to contribute to man's comfort and pleasure; or
it will add to the misery and unhappiness of the
-world as the honor or the greed of men shall dic-

tate. Its development depends upon the principles which the coming years will unfold.

The inventions of the present century have not only excelled those of any preceding century in number and importanuce, but it would not be a very great exaggeration to say that they equal those of all the preceding centuries combined. Have they added to the general well being and happiness of mankind in proportion to their number and importance? What has been the object, or motive, of all these inventions? Has it been the happiness of mankind or the making of money? Every one, even those with half wit, will say that the purpose of all these inventions was to make money. If the happiness of mankind entered into the calculation it was only as a purchasable quantity to be attained by a sufficient outlay of dollars and cents for the use of the invention. It would not be surprising then if mankind in general had been injured instead of having been benefited by the multiplicity of inventions.

Machines have lowered the prices of products, but they have at the same time curtailed the purchasing power by diminishing the opportunities of employment.

Wages are reported higher in late years; but it will be found that this is true only of those trades in which wages are sustained by strong unions. These trades unions alone have saved the labor market of America from degenerating into a slave market. The statistics on wages are not altogether reliable. We cannot judge of the state of wages gained by the mass of toilers from some selected industry or establishment. The wages paid in some prosperous establishment, where the employees belong to trades unions, will present a very favorable comparison with past years, but will the total wages paid to labor throughout the country show an increase in keeping with the growth of the population when compared with the conditions that prevailed before labor-saving machinery was so extensively used?

Labor has not profited by the invention and use of labor-saving machinery; it has suffered and very extensively. To improve the condition of labor wages should be higher, the hours should be shorter, or work should be abundant; but not one of these is absolutely true.

Some claim that wages are higher. They are in some trades, but they are not the effect of the use of labor-saving machinery, but the result of trades unions. Without unions and federations operators in every branch of industry would be in a most pitiable condition today. The over supply and consequent competition would have reduced wages below the starvation point without these unions. Before the advent of labor-saving devices farm hands received twenty-five or thirty dollars a month; now they do not receive more than one-half that amount; clerks in stores work for three or four dollars a week; typewriters and bookkeepers work for four or five dollars a week; garment makers work for five or six dollars a week; miners make four or five dollars a week, because employment is so scarce and the supply of labor so abundant that people are glad to get even these low wages.

The use of machinery has increased the hours of labor;* and if the hours are shorter in any

*"The Decorator and Furnisher."

branch of industry, it is because laws have restricted them, or because labor unions have forced employers to concede them. Where the supply of labor is over abundant wages are inevitably lowered and the hours are lengthened, unless these are maintained by moral power or by positive laws.

There is no room for argument on the subject of the abundance of work. The hundreds of thousands of idle men and women tell more strongly than any other argument that labor saving machines have ruined the labor market and have diminished the means of obtaining a livelihood.

We might divide all the inventions of the century into two classes; those that add to the comfort and happiness of mankind in general, and those which lessen the cost of production by displacing labor. The former are not necessarily the offspring of beneficent minds and intended solely to add to the sum of human happiness. They may be mercenary in their inspiration as well as the latter, but their originators did not aim at financial reward by forcing men from remunerative fields of labor. They add to the comforts and happiness of life without increasing the sum of human miseries and want. These mark the progress of the human race in the march of civilization. Those other inventions which do not perform any operation that cannot be done just as well, or even better, by hand and whose only purpose is to displace labor and lessen the cost of production, merely mark man's progress in rapacity and greed. They are not symbols of civilization because they violate the rights of mankind to the means of obtaining a livelihood, and because they diminish the means of procuring happiness.

Labor has not profited in any measure by labor-saving inventions. Labor-saving machines have greatly diminished the demand for skilled labor. Now boys or laborers may tend machines and do the work that formerly required skilled mechanics. Dull monotony has superceded skilled variety. Intelligence is no longer necessary in turning out fine work; machines supply the skill and anybody can tend to the machine. A monotonous uniform motion is all that is required to supply many machines with material; there is no call or room for the exercise of intelligence, and it is not surprising, as an observer remarked, that men take to drink as soon as the day's work is done.

Poor wages, less requirements of intelligence and skill in operators have served to degrade, morally and socially, those employed in manufacturing by machine systems. High wages as the reward of skill would command respect and would give labor a standing in the community.

Our merchants and manufacturers boast of being able to undersell European producers in their own market, even in those lines of goods of which they were supposed to have a monopoly either by reason of their long experience or their cheap labor. Our inventors have studied not only to displace labor by machinery but have also directed their genius to increasing the efficiency of machinery by multiplying the operations without an addition of time. Machines will drill a dozen holes in the same time that they would formerly drill one, and this increase of efficiency has lessened most perceptibly the cost of production.

Formerly our statesmen claimed that American workmen could not compete with foreign cheap labor; now English manufacturers say that American cheap labor is ruining their business, and they must lower wages if they wish to hold their trade.* New inventions to increase the producing power of machines, displacing labor or otherwise lessening the cost of production, place our manufacturers at an advantage over their English rivals.

We are proud of our vast foreign trade, but it is being secured at the sacrifice of industrial prosperity which should constitute the nation's honor. We can undersell European cheap labor in their home markets because we substitute machines for men. If wealth** is of more account than the happiness of men, then we are on the

---

*This is the answer of manufacturers to the labor representatives in the present great strike of engineers and steel workers in England.

**Wealth threatens to dominate mankind in the future as tyranny did in the past. Morris, "Civilization."

high road to commercial supremacy and are lead-
ing the van of a new civilization.

Civilization has its ebb and flow like the tides,
as in the different periods of human history men
are controlled by some dominant idea. The an-
cients surpassed us in literature and sculpture,
and the painting of today is not up to the standard of past centuries. We have had a stone age
and an iron age, and it looks now as if we were to
have a machine age. Machines are substituted
in every possible way for men; and some seem
to think that this is the symbol of our civilization, accomplishing greater results with less
effort. Fine arts are no longer the product of
genius, skill and patient toil; they are now made
by machines. Raffael, Rubens, and Firatorel
were poor benighted beings of the dark ages who
labored long months on one work; now machines
can stamp thousands of our high grade art paint-
ings in a day! What need of a Paderewski, a
Rubenstein, a Wilhelmj in this progressive age?
Have we not our steam calliope that will grind
out music in unlimited quantities, and it only
needs fuel and, perhaps, a little oil occasionally

to keep it going? We have our hand organ and street pianos that only need a strong arm to turn out ceaseless music Greater production at less cost! Behold the spirit of the age, the symbol of fin de siecle civilization!

There is ample field for all the inventive genius of the world to discover the still hidden powers of nature and subordinate them to the uses of men without inventing machines to take bread from the mouth of the poor, increasing the poverty and adding to the sum of human misery. Cities may be beautified, homes may be adorned and the comforts, conveniences and happiness of mankind may be increased a hundred fold by inventions yet to come. The principles of light and heat are not yet fully understood or reduced to practical forms; the uses to which electricity may be put are still in the region of the unknown; medicine and the art of conserving human life are still in embryo; and there are mysterious powers still hidden in nature's great storehouse awaiting the explorer's coming to be added to the grandeur of the triumph of the genius of man.

Inventions which add to the comfort, pleasure and happiness of mankind, without throwing men out of employment, are the true symbols of progress and civilization. Among the more recent ones of this class may be mentioned the bicycle and the barrel shaped churn. The bicycle has not displaced anyone in the field of labor. It has given employment to half a million of men in the different branches of manufacture and sale. Without it half a million more would have been added to the idle toilers in the past year, to walk the streets looking for work. It may have taken some of the traffic* from the railways, but the general public will not consider this a loss. The churn has been a great blessing to the farmer's wife, upon whom generally devolved the task of making butter; and it has taken away much of the hardship from an irksome task.

Inventions which do not add to the means of comfort and happiness of the general public and

*The bicycle has not to any extent taken the place of the horse and carriage. At the twenty-fifth annual convention of the Carriage Builders' Association, N. Y., Oct., 1897, it was the opinion: "The substitution of the bicycle for the carriage has been such only to a limited extent, and the harm done to our trade is nominal."

which serve no other purpose than to add to the revenue of a few individuals by displacing labor, and adding to the general distress, should be either prohibited by law or should be taxed to the full amount of labor displaced. They contribute nothing to the true civilization, progress or happiness of the world. They breed anarchy and discontent by depriving the toilers of the means of procuring happiness, and offer unjust advantages to those using them to grow rich at the expense of the poor.

If it is the first duty of a civilized government to protect its subjects in their rights to the means of happiness, it is the duty of that government to prohibit the use of inventions which absorb or destroy those means. A free government will not do this through paternal instinct or a sense of honor, but it may be forced to adopt these just principles through the concerted actions of its interested citizens. There is ample field for the employment of inventive genius in developing methods for beautifying the world and rendering more easy the lot of human life without inventing methods of taking bread from the poor man's mouth, and government sanction should not be given, through the patent office, to those inventions whose only purpose is to enrich a few at the expense of the multitudes, and which are opposed to the general welfare of the great mass of people.

CHAPTER VII.

LAWS AND LAW-MAKING.

Law, at one time, meant an ordinance established by lawful authority for the public good. Law is still a sacred guide to the common people; and they believe it to be what nature intended it should be, a reflection of the Divine mind ruling the world. If the public good were the object of all legislative and municipal law, then the people of the United States should be the most happy and prosperous in the world. The people send their representatives to the Congress, to the state legislatures, and to the city councils, and all these diligently labor for several months each year in passng laws for the guidance of the people.

It does seem passing strange that with all these numerous law-making bodies, and their rapid transit facilities for turning out laws, that the public should be in such a pitiable plight, and that lamentations should be heard throughout the land instead of peons of praise and thanksgiving. Is it possible that prosperity is not de-

pendent upon the will of man, and that it cannot bo conjured into being by human law? Do
not all these law-makers sacrifice their time to
serve their country and their fellow men, and do
they not keep before their eyes continually the
great aim of all their labors, the good of their
country and the welfare of their fellow men?

Whenever the land was threatened by foreign
invaders, or by internal foes, thousands of brave
men left their homes to defend their country.
Patriotism does not depend upon the bloody carnage of war for its life. Men can serve their
country in peace as well as in war, in the legislative hall as well as on the field of battle. Men
are even more eager to serve their country in
official capacity in time of peace than in war;
but is the magnet that draws them the love of
country and their fellow men or the love of gold?

A history of legislation in our national capital,
in our state legislature, and in our city councils
might reveal the sordid motives which animate
our statesmen in the framing of our innumerable
laws. The unselfish patriotism of our fathers
has vanished from the land. No man now seeks

public office except from selfish motives. Men once served their country from a sense of honor, and devoted their time and talents to the interests of their fellow men. If all this is changed now it is not because men have deteriorated, but because conditions have changed, and instead of the Goddess of Justice, or the Goddess of Love, being the symbol of the spirit that guides our law-making bodies, it is the spirit of Evil, or Mammon.

Individuals and great corporations long ago learned that they could secure very valuable franchises and privileges through laws passed by the representatives of the people; and as these privileges were worth enormous sums of money, when measured according to market values, men were ready to buy them, or buy the means of obtaining them; and when the law-makers found that their votes were worth large sums of money, which could be obtained without any apparent sacrifice of honor, it was quite natural that they should adopt this means of increasing their income or acquiring a fortune. In nearly all legislative bodies rings are formed under the

control of corporations or individuals to secure
laws conferring exclusive and valuable privileges, which are merely a transfer of public right
to private title; and any individual member of
such body of probity and honor cannot obtain
the passage of any law, however just and necessary it might be, unless he works with the ring
in some disreputable scheme. This may seem
to some like unjust accusations, or like the grue-
some theory of a pessimist who cannot see any
brightness in life or honor in men; but the fact
is so patent it scarcely needs proof.

St. Clair McKelway, editor of the Brooklyn
Eagle, in his address at the graduating exercises
of Union College, this year,* made the following
caustic reference to the sale of legislation: "The
nation which abolished the sale of human beings
is being accustomed to the sale of law .. .. Our
legislatures of all grades are becoming expert
practitioners of this evil. The venality of aldermen is a proverb. The corruption of boards of
supervisors is a habit. The ownership of legislatures is constantly in evidence. The assault of

*1897.

landed interests, affected by a money relation to law, upon Congress, terrorizes the timid, scandalizes the moral and appals the thoughtful. The illicit getting of money by political bosses for political purposes has been reduced to a system which has enabled these bosses absolutely to create legislatures and congresses elected to deal with the very iniquities to which they owe their existence. The corporations which these collectors of blackmail have successfully assaulted seek compensation out of the public treasury by privileges and monopolies enacted by boughten laws."

A conservative journal, in editorial comment of this address, says: "No one questions the influence of wealth in legislative halls, and in the minds of many thoughtful persons it constitutes the chief danger of the American Republic. Only the most persistent optimist will assert that there is any visible improvement in this respect from year to year. The evil grows in magnitude, and must eventually threaten popular government, if not checked."

The privileges which are granted to individuals and corporations by legislative enactment are rights of the people which could not in justice be alienated without proper compensation to the owners. Robbery is the unjust taking away of one's property by violence; and theft is the taking away of the same by stealth: but the conferring of valuable privileges embracing the property and rights of the public, without adequate compensation contains all the moral iniquity of each of these crimes without the risk of contracting the legal guilt of either.

Men who take part in legislation which helps to enrich themselves by defrauding the public are not looked upon as dishonorable or dishonest; and they mingle in society as respectable members of the community, their success often being a passport to exclusive circles. It is true that public opinion is occasionally aroused to such a pitch that officials are forced to send a few aldermen to prison; but the awful dignity of higher legislators surrounds their personality with invisible protection, something like the divinity that doth hedge a king, and shields them from any imputation of venality.

When men have learned to stifle any qualms of conscience in the conduct of public affairs, it is but a step further to introduce the same principles in their private business. Money is becoming more and more the standard of men's worth; and the millionaires of every town belong to the inner circle of the "best people." No question is asked regarding the methods by which men have acquired wealth. The fact of its legal existence overawes the public, and commands, at least openly, the respect which the world bestows upon greatness.

The country could dispense with the services of many of its law-making bodies for long periods, with profit to its prosperity; for our honorable legislators no longer serve their country, but they are the humble servants of trusts, of corporations and political rings. The success of their public career depends upon their fidelity to party principles. Party principles are a combination of good and evil: some good public policy, to catch the public eye and gain votes;

and the passage of iniquitous laws that will bring money into their coffers, either directly or through the trusts in whose interests these laws are passed.

Patriotism pays poorly in these days. It will reward its devotees with honor and fame; but a man cannot live in style and comfort on these. Trusts pay well in current money, and money is as necessary for the life of political rings and parties as it is for the individual. We are not surprised, then, to find the granting of valuable franchises made a party issue;* for in this way parties repay the trusts for enormous contributions to campaign expenses. The trusts and the political rings have mutual interests, and both thrive by preying on the people. Yet this is a free country, and this is a government of the people, for the people, by the people! It is about time for the people to be awakened from their

*Two rival corporations in New York City were recently struggling to obtain a valuable franchise from the aldermen, and each corporation had the backing of one of the two great parties. The franchise meant money and votes to the successful party.

lethargy, and be taught to assume their prerogatives.

Americans are patriotic and law-abiding. They love their country and are disposed to obey all her laws. They do not stop to question the methods that have been employed to pass laws that infringe on their rights, or that usurp their title, vested in the State, to public property. It is sufficient for them that a law has been passed by a legal law-making body, and they are willing to obey it.

If there are any wrongs in the labor problem that may be righted by legislation, or any change beneficial to labor that may be effected by law, the remedy lies in the hands of the toilers. The toilers should be able to control every legislative body in the United States. It is the only method that offers any hope of success, and they do not understand their own interests if they do not make use of this facile means of promoting them. The idea that party politics would destroy the harmony of trades unions has been one of their fundamental principles, and, as they believed, one of their cardinal virtues. They need not have anything to do with party principles; their own interests are sufficiently vast to engage their whole attention. They may leave office hunting, except legislative, and spoils-hunting, as well as party principles, to the political hacks and party machines. They should not consider any principle or policy which does not directly effect their own interests. In this way mere politics will be excluded from their meetings; but they will make a fatal mistake if they do not aim to secure legislative power.*

*Edward Harford, who with Havelock Wilson, M. P., constituted the British Trades Unions delegation to the Nashville convention of the American Federation of Labor, sailed for Southampton on the American liner St. Paul today. Before sailing, Mr. Harford said: "The policy of the American Trades Unions in not engaging in politics as a body is stupid. How can they expect to obtain any lasting reforms if they hold aloof? By pursuing their present mummy plan of ignoring the control of political machinery as a means of bettering their condition, they are not only fatally ignoring their chances, but are inviting the scorn of the politicians—the very class from whom they expect to get better laws for the masses. Your American politician, as a rule, is moved into legislation for the masses only by show of superior force. Let the trades unions force this style of puppet into retirement and send men to boards of Aldermen, Legislatures and Congress who will not pretend to be the friends of the people in speeches and in secret sell out to the corporations and money power."

When we consider the millions upon millions expended every year upon legislative bodies in the United States, we must conclude that America is the best governed country in the world. The United States expends probably more upon legislation than any country in the world. Members are elected to make laws, and each one feels that the responsibility of his position and his duties to his constituents, require him to have at least one law passed during his term. We have statutes on every conceivable subject, from the governmnt of the army to the regulation of fish and fowl.

There are about two hundred members in the New York State Legislature; and if every member has only one bill passed we will have at least two hundred new statutes each year. When we add to these the laws of Congress and municipal laws we can understand something of the thousands upon thousands of laws and statutes that are forced upon the forbearing citizens of the United States. Many of these laws are merely schemes to strengthen the party or plunder the public treasury; whilst others grant franchises to corporations, which legislators have no right to give without just compensation to the people.

The laws passed by the Legislature of the State of New York for the last one hundred years fill more than one hundred thousand pages of printed books; and every year about one hundred pages more are added to this vast volume of statute law. If these laws added to the comfort, happiness or well being of the citizens in general there might be some excuse for their vastness; but, as a rule, they only place intolerable burdens of taxation upon the many by granting special privileges to the few.

The great majority of the members of the legislature are young men who have made no special study of the science of government, and have no conception of the true needs of the country. They are young lawyers and business men whose ideal is the party leader; whose conception of duty is to serve the party that placed them in power, or to further the interests of corporations that will generously reward them.

In every business of great importance special training, or skill and experience, are necessary

for a successful career; but in law-making success depends upon ability to have bills passed,
and to keep in with the party leaders to secure
another term.

The science of government, especially as man-
ifested through our statute laws, has not kept in
line with the progress in every other branch of
science and art. Law has been a mere play-
thing in the hands of designing men; and government has been merely the instrument they
employed to further the interests of individuals,
corporations and parties. Law has been but a
wooden toy floating about on the bosom of the
mighty river of progress, borne along and tossed
about by the whirlpools and the eddies of con-
flicting human interests.

It seems strange how the country could prosper, in the early years of its history, with so
few laws. Laws are turned out now in such
quantities that the country is fairly overwhelmed
with them; and if numbers of laws and statutes
could make a people prosperous and happy this
should be the greatest country on the face of the
globe. The rush to the Klondike for gold is not

a greater manifestation of eager greed than is the zeal of the members of our law-making bodies to have bills passed—a display of misguided patriotism. The President and the Governors of the various states mercifully spare the country from the infliction of numberless harmful laws every year, by the exercise of their veto power or by allowing bills to die without their sanction.

Rotaiton in offices of the government are often beneficial to the country, because it brings new men and better methods to the work. Nearly the same class of men, having the same party affiliations and guided by the same principles, have been succeeding one another in the legislative bodies of the land for the past half century. The legislation favored by them and the laws they have passed have not brought prosperity to the land. An entire change of men and principles might benefit the country.

All agree that abundance of work for all at good wages would bring prosperity to the land. Present parties and principles have failed to bring back prosperous times. Party leaders or statesmen do not hold out any rational hope of improvement, do not offer any sensible solution of the problem.

Those in whose interests any legislation is proposed, should be best qualified to determine what elements would make it most beneficial and effective. The great mass of toilers, on the farms and in the shops, are the ones who are most directly interested in labor legislation, and they should have representatives in every law-making body. If the prosperity of the toilers, plenty of work at good wages, means the prosperity of the entire country, then permanent prosperity may come to the country through wise labor legislation.

Any measure which is within the realm of morality and justice, may become a law in the United States. The Constitution is the fundamental law of the land; but even this may be interpreted, modified or changed by the supreme will of the people. The will of the people, especially represented through party principles, may give a different meaning to laws; and the court interpretations of law will be biased towards the general desire.

The entire financial, industrial and commercial policy of the country may be changed or directed by law. If the present principles of parties are not favorable to prosperity, there must surely be brains enough in the land to direct affairs into a more healthful channel. If the past class of legislators has not been successful in keeping prosperity in the land why not try another? The great mass of toilers has never been adaquately represented in our legislatures. They may not be so well educated or so intelligent as the party and machine men; but they should know their own wants and their interests, and their interests are the foundation of prosperity. It is not absolutely necessary that men from their ranks should be in legislative halls. They might secure men of ability and education to represent their interests, even though these did not belong to their ranks.* There are plenty of honorable men, who have never taken active part in politics, who could be induced to serve the interests of their country and their fellow men.

*Money foolishly squandered in strikes would be far better employed in securing legislation.

Enormous sums of money are spent in our election campaigns. Where does all this money come from? It comes from individuals who are looking for favors from the government; it comes from the trusts that combine, under government protection, to uphold prices, whilst they starve their operatives; it comes from the great corporations that enjoy franchises and privileges worth untold millions and that are looking for more. Corporations have an eye to business; and they do not contribute to any political party except they have good prospect of getting the full value of their money, in the continued enjoyment of present privileges, or promises of further largesses.

Candidates for public office are now obliged by law to make a sworn statement of their election expenses. Why could we not go a step further and make it a misdemeanor to contribute to the campaign fund? All the necessary and legitimate election expenses are born by the State; the corruption fund comes from those who intend to recover from the coffers of the State.

CHAPTER VIII.

One of the most important subjects that government is called upon to deal with is taxation. A patriotic people are willing to contribute generously of their earnings to the support of government; and in return the civil authorities secure them in the peaceful possession of prosperity and the rational enjoyment of life.

In olden times rapine and war were the means selected to sustain the dignity of the king or defray the expenses of the ruling power. Feudalism, estates of the realm, the tributes of dependent princes and provinces, were the successive systems adopted to contribute towards government support. The present principles of taxing all according to the wealth and ability of every man is one of the results of the recognition of the rights of the individual and the extension of the right of suffrage.

The present system of taxing property, real and personal, is universal throughout the United States; yet it is only in recent years that the methods became nearly uniform, and even now there is much diversity in details and in the objects subject to taxation. Real and personal property were selected as the objects of taxation because these were believed to most faithfully represent the ability of the individual to contribute towards the support of government; but it is very difficult to reach personal property, and those possessing the greatest amount are but rarely contributors to the town or state treasury.

A great amount of wealthy people's investments is exempt by Federal law from State taxation; and much more is so evanescent and illusory that it escapes the scrutiny of argus-eyed assessors. United States bonds are exempt from taxation, and stocks of various kinds are of such intangible value and illusory nature that the State is never able to trace their ownership or derive any revenue from their existence.

Several states* have attempted to demand tribute from this class of property by inheritance tax laws; but the power and influence of

*New York, Pennsylvania, etc.

wealth strives to illude these laws by legal con-
tention.* Death reveals the hordes of wealth
that have been unscrupulously hidden from the
State; and the latter secures the peaceful trans-
mission of enormous sums to legal heirs, and is
rewarded for the intervention of its power by
the refusal of this class of wealth to pay its just
dues. Much of this class of property could not
subsist, or be safely transmitted to legal heirs
without the protection of the courts, which secure the living in their peaceful possession and
give sanction and effect to the will of the dead.

Greed overawes patriotism and every other
civic virtue, and men will only render their just
tribute to government by the strict enforcement
of positive laws. Men who have accumulated
enormous riches under the fostering care of
national and state laws absolutely refuse to contribute to the support of the power which has
been a necessary element in the production of
their wealth. Wealth brings power and influ-

*Some judges (Ashway, Ferguson, etc.) have
declared inheritance tax laws unconstitutional,
whilst others have held that they are valid; and
the question will probably be referred to the Supreme Court.

ence; and rich men often use these two to shirk their own responsibility, and to force the burdens of government sustenance upon the shoulders of the poor; yet the fundamental idea of our tax is based on the theory that men should contribute towards the support of the government in proportion to their ability; yet most reforms in the tax laws tend more and more to throw these burdens upon the consuming power of the land, and as the poor form the greater portion of the consumers, being the more numerous, taxes eventually fall upon their shoulders.

One hundred years ago there was very little personal property in the United States; and a tax upon realty constituted a very fair form of assessment upon the ability of individuals to contribute to government support. The growth of personal property has kept pace with the growth of wealth until, at present, it has attained enormous proportions in the land. The value of personal property in the most thickly settled states is equal to the real estate, yet the greater portion of personal property escapes taxation. The New York assessors maintain that the personal property of the state fully equals in value the real estate, yet it only pays twelve per cent. of the amount of taxes.*

A tax on personal property is correct and apparently simple in principle, but it has not been found practicable in any state or municipality.** Personal property is too intangible, too easily transferred, too illusory, to be a proper object of taxation; but if it could be reached it would constitute a very fair form of taxation.

Authorities do not agree on the meaning of direct and indirect taxation; but a pretty clear definition is that, direct taxes are those which fall upon a person's property and business; the indirect taxes are those which are placed upon articles, such as food, clothing, and other objects of commerce. An indirect tax in this sense would seem to fall most heavily upon those who are least able to bear the burden. The vast majority of consumers of ordinary articles are the poor, and the things necessary for daily life and comfort should be free from taxes, and should

*Report, 1881.

**"Taxation in the United States," Ely.

be placed, as far as possible, within the reach of all.*

It is not a very easy matter to devise a just and thoroughly effective system of taxation. Some claim that the power of production constitutes the only theoretically just basis of taxation. Men are bound to serve the State, they say, in the same degree in which they have ability to serve themselves. Some** believe that, in the ultimate analysis, land is the only real producer; and, consequently, a tax upon land is the only equitable and comprehensive method of assessment, but in the complicated branches of modern business life there are many sources of wealth which do not seem to have any relation to land.

All admit that men should be taxed according to their wealth, or their ability, and the only difficulty in practice is to determine the amount of each citizen's ability. The great food producing branch of industry, agriculture, is taxed; not indeed as a producing power, but as real es-

*Walker.
**Henry George.

tate. Other forms of production, such as manufactures, are not taxed except they are holders or renters of realty; and they are even granted immunities and privileges as fostering elements of prosperity. Why should these forms of producing power be exempt from taxation, unless, indeed, it is claimed for them that they are necessary for the public weal? If, however, they are not only not necessary for the public weal, but are actually, under present methods, the cause of industrial depression, who will say that they should not be adequately, and even heavily, taxed?

Every branch of productive industry in which labor-saving machinery has been introduced suffers from the ill effects of overproduction. Overproduction is at the bottom of every industrial depression. The aim of the producers has been to lessen the cost and to increase the products; and the inventive genius of the country has turned out four or five thousand improved machines each year to accomplish these results. The inevitable results followed: labor was displaced; the consuming power was lessened; the market was glutted; the hum of industry was stilled because there was no demand; the toiler could not buy, because he had no work; stagnation and gloom settled on the land. These are not the creations of disordered imaginations, the ravings of an anarchist, nor the dark forboding of a pessimist, but they are cold facts taken from observation and from the industrial history of the world, and which anyone may verify by opening his eyes to the light and by observing the phenomena everywhere patent.

Tariff tinkering and finance juggling will never remedy the ills of industry. These have about as much influence on the prosperity of the country as the tricks of a thimble rigger at a county fair have on agriculture. The laws of supply and demand govern industry, and when these are in a healthful condition prosperity will smile upon the land without any favors from nation or state. The government can assist by regulating supply and demand, and by reducing them, when either is in extraordinary excess, to healthful conditions. This is the proper province of Government, and it is what the United States practically attempts to do by its system of tariff for the protection of home industries; but this can never bring prosperity because it is fostering the very evil it is intended to suppress.

In nearly every branch of manufacture and production the products are far in excess of home consumption; and our merchants and manufacturers are looking for markets in South America, in Europe, and in Asia, for their surplus goods. Conservative men estimate that enough goods can be produced in three months, with present methods, to supply the home market for one year. Under old methods of hand work, it would require, according to one of our most competent authorities,* from fifty to one hundred million of workers to produce the amount of goods that may be manufactured by the present facilities of labor-saving machinery, with the present working force of eight or nine millions.

The present system** of taxation is compara-

*Carroll D. Wright, head of the Government Bureau of Labor.

**Ely, "Taxation in American States."

tively new, dating back no farther than the time of the Civil War, and even at the present time there is great diversity of methods of taxation in the different states and cities. Pennsylvania levies a tax on foreign insurance companies, on bankers and brokers, on saving institutions and express companies. All cities grant licenses, which are but certificates of taxes paid on the particular business for which they are issued. Charleston, S. C., taxes fifty-six different kinds of business. Before the Civil War there was a poll tax, and individuals were also taxed according to their earning capacity.

In 1895 a bill was passed by the United States Congress which proposed to levy a tax upon the incomes of individuals. It was intended to assess individuals according to their ability; in proportion as they were able to serve themselves, so would they be required to serve the government. A limit was placed on this tax, so that its burden would not fall upon the poor, or those least able to bear it. Interested parties had the bill placed immediately on the calendar of the United States Supreme Court where it was declared unconstitutional. No event of recent years has dealt such a heavy blow at the patriotism of America's loyal subjects as this decision of her highest tribunal of justice. People were wont to look with pride to the Supreme Court of the United States, because they believed it was far removed from the corrupting influences of power and wealth;* but the decision has led them to believe that their idol has feet of common clay.

The tax on imported goods as a measure of government support is another evidence of the injustice of the method which places all the burden upon the poor. It was intended as a protection to home industries, by practically excluding many foreign goods from competing with our home products. This should protect home manufacturers in their business, and give steady employment to men. This seems specious enough in theory, but in practice it throws the whole tax upon the poor and increases the earn-

*Senator Vest said, the decision shows the power of money and monopoly. Justice Harlan was very much opposed to the decision, and strongly favored the minority opinion.

ings of the home producers. Senator Butler's arraignment of its injustice is very near the truth. "The tariff imposes its burden upon the ninety-eight per cent. of poor people who are least able to bear it, whilst it benefits the two per cent. of those who do not need assistance."*

Protective tariff laws may give a fitful boom to home industries by increasing the prospective profits of home products, but this revival is founded on the supposition that our home market is now invaded by foreign cheap goods. The truth is that American cheap goods are now flooding all the accessible markets of the world; and new labor-saving methods are being constantly introduced to enable our manufacturers to increase their products without adding to the number of their employees. If the object of the tariff laws was to create a greater demand for labor, the promoters exerted their zeal in the wrong direction. To cure an ill you must remove the cause; and the cause of the impotent demand for labor is the enormous displacement of the same by labor-saving machinery.

*Speech in U. S. Senate.

A little over a century ago a new school of political economy flourished in France, whose principal tenet was, that agriculture is the only productive industry. Vast estates then monopolized the land, excluded men from the use of the soil, which was the principal means of earning a livelihood there, and brought poverty and suffering upon the toiling masses. To correct this evil the French Economists proposed to abolish all tax except that upon land.

The revolution came and upset theories and schools; overturned dynasties; and abolished the class that absorbed the means of living. Men would not listen to reason; they were obliged to yield to force. Napoleon compelled the large land owners to place their large estates upon the market. They were divided up into millions of small farms, and France became one of the most prosperous and contented countries in the world.

The single tax theory has been revived* in the United States of late years, and many look upon it as a remedy for existing ills. The evil, how-

* This is the theory of Henry George.

ever, in the United States is not agrarian; it is industrial. One hundred years ago agriculture might have been reasonably looked upon as the only productive industry; but modern conditions have made possible numberless methods of combinations and change, and the finished products of the past century are only the crude materials of today. Hundreds of forms of wealth and methods of attaining wealth are in existence today that were unknown a century ago, and the single tax is too limited for the complications of modern business. Our ordinary land-owning farmer is the poorest paid toiler, whilst our men of greatest wealth and greatest ability of producing wealth may possess but little land.

There is no monopoly of land in the United States. Farms may be purchased, even in the Empire State, almost for a song. Land grabbing in cities and suburbs, where there is promise of enormous "unearned increments,"* is, as a rule, carefully watched and assessed according

---

*The principle of "unearned increment" enters into every branch of business that is dependant upon a valuable market. The merchant or broker buys larger quantities of goods—sugar,

to value; and this form of speculation is, in any case, exposed to great risks, and is liable to bring disaster as well as wealth. Credit should be given to good judgment in this as well as in every other form of business enterprise.

Although there is no monopoly of land in this country there is just as baneful a monopoly, a monopoly of the methods of production; machines are monopolizing the work of men. The single tax theory was founded on the principle that ability to produce should be the measure of taxation. There is no valid reason why this principle should be applied to agriculture alone; for land merely produces the crude material, in many branches of modern industry, and it derives the lowest percentage of profit from the finished products of all those through whose hands it passes in its progress towards completion. If ability to produce is the true basis of taxation, as many believe, the principle should

tea, cloth, oil or stocks; the price for reasons over which he has no control, rises, and he reaps the profits of the "unearned increment." Henry George himself profited by "unearned increment." His writings—his books, his paper, had a money value which was given to them by the reading public.

be applied to all stages in the process of completion which add value to the product. Not only the farmer should be taxed who raises the flax, the sheep for wool, cotton or the cocoon as raw materials, but also the manufacturers who convert these into valuable materials for clothing; and these should be taxed according to their ability to produce with labor-saving machinery in proportion to their displacement of hand labor, because in the same proportion they have absorbed the means from which the laboring classes derive the power to contribute towards government support.

There is a tendency, especially in the smaller towns, to donate lands as sites for manufactories, and to offer other inducements to manufacturers to locate and build, on the supposition that their presence would add to the prosperity of the place by giving employment to idle hands. Men have a general idea that increasing the demand for labor will add to prosperity; then why not abolish by taxation the use of labor-saving machinery, which is the direct cause of the enormous displacement of labor? Granting privileges to manufactories is only fostering the very evil which should be eradicated, and which is causing the "hard times" and scarcity of work.

The existence of manufactories using labor-saving machinery is unfavorable to the growth of small towns. The division of labor, propinquity to large markets, and facility of securing desirable employees, favorably incline the manufacturers towards the large cities. Before the advent of the modern factory every town kept busy its own shoemakers and tailors, but now these are supplanted by the ready-to-wear clothes and the machine-made shoes. Fifteen or twenty years ago there were many prosperous little towns in Kansas and throughout other states of the Central West; but today they are only represented by the deserted brick block or the deserted school; they have been effaced from the earth; machines, like the plague locusts, nipped them in the bud.

There is a general impression that under our present system of taxation, property owners alone pay taxes, and the "taxpayer" claims the right to be heard on all questions where the expenditure of public money is involved. As a matter of fact, however, the property owner manages to make others pay his taxes; and in its last analysis the whole burden of taxation falls upon the non-property owning consumer. If taxes are increased, the landlord will raise the rent of the poor man's dwelling in the same ratio; if it is business property, the price of goods will be raised to meet the increased taxation. The consumer pays a few cents more for his tea, and his coffee, or his sugar; a few shillings more for his household goods, his household clothes or his shoes; and this added cost goes to pay the merchants, or the landlord's increased taxation.

The landlord calculates to get ten per cent. gross on his capital invested in rentable realty; so that he may pay his taxes and insurance and a little for repairs, and then realize six per cent. net from his investment. The merchant calculates his expenses, his employee's wages, his rent or his taxes, his heating and lighting expense, his advertising, his insurance, and he adds all these to the cost of his goods; and then he will add his own prospective profit, and thus he makes up the selling price of his goods. In each case the consumer pays the taxes, and the great mass of consumers are the poor workers who own no real estate or visible taxable property.

No one believes that it is just right to saddle the burden of government support upon the backs of the poor; yet the tendency of recent legislation and of official and business methods has been in this direction.

There is a widespread and growing belief that present systems of taxation are unjust, and do not place the burdens upon those who are best able to bear them, and where they properly belong. Reforms in tax laws are proposed in various legislatures; the objects which should pay tribute to government form the subject of discussion; and in the final settlement of this question the great mass of consumers, who, under the present system pay the heaviest proportionate taxes, should have a prominent part. If the matter is left to the great parties, professional politicians, and law makers to decide, they will favor the great corporations and the trusts that can contribute abundantly to party support.

CHAPTER IX.
REMEDIES.

In all the great manufacturing countries of the world there have been recurrent periods of financial and industrial depression; whilst an even tenor of stability, disturbed only by crop failures, outside of the United States, has been the fortune of agricultural lands. Agriculture has also suffered periods of depression; but it has been through the seemingly absurd paradox of over abundance. When the markets are over supplied with food products or manufactured goods prices must fall; and the slump affects not only the owner of products, but also all those engaged in their production.

In the United States, in England, in Germany, in France, and in some of the other nations of Europe there have been periods of financial flurry and panics, often accompanied or followed by industrial depressions; but in most cases these are of slight duration, and have not silenced the hum of industry or checked the prosperity of the land. These panics

are caused either by excessive speculation in
finances or over-production in industry; and
when they are caused by the former the sober
senses of men will soon adjust affairs to healthful conditions; but when they are caused by
the latter then men must patiently wait until
the consuming power of the world has exhausted the supply and makes a new demand.

Statesmen, political economists, ordinary
politicians, and merchants, like learned physi-
cians, have examined all the inductive conditions and present symptoms, have made a scientific diagnosis, have prescribed a compound of
new-made tariff for the nerves, a proper proportion of gold and silver solution to strengthen
the spine, and have issued their wise prognosis
for the comfort of the patient's friends; yet the
sick still languish; the learned men have been
misled by symptoms.

The money question is the most absurd and
ridiculous issue that has ever been presented to
the American people at a presidential election.
Financial flurries are generally only symptoms
of industrial distress. As well hope to cure

epilepsy by assisting a fellow victim to his feet as to expect to remedy industrial depression by financial legislation. Give men work at fair wages and every financial difficulty will soon disappear. There is no question about what kind of money we shall use; but the vital question is, whether the great mass of workers shall have an opportunity of earning any kind of money. The kind of money we shall use has about as much bearing upon the prosperity of the country as has the social question, whether bicycle women shall wear bloomers. The great leaders of either party have eloquently expounded the value of their nostrums, but their effusions seem like mere chaff blown from the political machines to hoodwink the people.

If men are once firmly convinced of the true causes of "hard times," or industrial depression, there are surely patriotism and humanity enough in America to arouse them to the necessity of providing a remedy. Men, however, are not easily influenced by considerations of patriotism or humanity when these clash with their monetary interests; and the great trusts and monopolies would no doubt throw the weight of their power and wealth against any proposition which would tend to weaken their influence or lessen their gains. Unequivocal laws strictly enforced that might be introduced for the public good will do more to induce these corporations to submit to new, and perhaps unfavorable conditions than any thought of country or their fellow men.

The great corporations and trusts have been able, for many years, to control legislation in nearly all the law-making bodies in the United States. They soon learned that the road to wealth led through legislative halls rather than through business marts, and their immense power and money were directed towards securing immunities, privileges, laws and franchises that were worth untold millions to them.

These were generally free gifts secured through bribery, encroachment upon the public domain or were valuable franchises secured without adequate compensation The people virtually own the streets of towns, the highways of the country, and all public property;

and legislative-governing bodies are mere guardians of the peoples' rights and property. The law-making bodies* of the United States have been infamously corrupt for some years, and have bartered away the peoples' birthright for a mess of potage.

The great glory of this country is that it is a government of the people, for the people, and by the people. This is true in theory, but in fact the great glory of the land has long since departed, and for years it has been a government of the great corporations and trusts by the politicians, for gain. The power of governing still resides in the people, but it lies dormant, and it has been usurped by parties organized for plunder. Much good for the permanent prosperity of the country can be effected by the people resuming their original rights. How can this be done?

Each of the great political parties is equally immersed in corruption and exists principally for spoil; and even if a new party were formed it would soon fall a victim to the wiles of Mam-

*See Chapter VII.

mon. The great mass of the people are too busy earning a living and attending to business affairs to give any time or thought to practical politics. This gives a clear field to the politicians, who have only to struggle among themselves for the offices and the spoils.* There is practically no check on the corruption in politics, or on the abuse of legislative power. A strong, efficient, yet simple means of removing corrupt politicians from office and which could brand them with infamy would effect much good for the country, and could also by legislation correct many of the evils in the industrial world.

All through the country workmen are united in unions for the protection and promotion of their interests. They have been fairly successful in maintaining wages in some branches, whilst in others they have failed. They may strike; but as long as the supply of labor,

*These spoils are enormous. "As things are now," said ex-Gov. Altgeld in his Labor Day speech, "the people have to bear the burden of corruption among officials, have to fatten a lot of politicians and have to fill the coffers of insatiable corporations besides."

skilled in the strikers' trade, is greatly in excess of the demand the struggle will be unequal, and they will surely lose. If the demand for labor can be increased to such an extent that it will exceed the supply, then there will be no need for a strike, because it will be to the employers' interests to comply with the employees demands; or if there is need for a strike they may hope for success. This may sound simple enough, in fact it seems self-evident, but how can the change be effected?

Labor has been losing ground, because it has not been guided by intelligence. It has been like a great powerful animal, bellowing in rage at its captivity and its captors, whilst it is being shackled by a tiny mite of physical power endowed with reason. In all the progress of the present century labor has not profited in any perceptible measure, simply because it has not known how to take advantage of the opportunities offered. They toil today in the fields and in the shops much as they did one hundred years ago. They have machines, 'tis true, to co-operate with them, but these machines are not intended to take the burden of toil from their shoulders, they even add to it by substituting insufferable sameness for pleasing variety. The principal and about the only purpose of the use of machinery is to lessen the cost of production and manufacture and to make the rich richer. The condition of labor has not improved with the manifold wonderful invention of the present century; it has not kept pace with progress.

The policy of redressing their grievances, or of improving their condition by strikes is becoming more hopeless every day. Men leave their work and go on strike on the principle that employers will pay higher wages sooner than allow their works to remain idle; but in most cases, other workers may be easily secured to take the strikers' places, and as long as this condition prevails strikes will prove failures.

Strikes were all right enough in the past century, or even thirty or forty years ago before labor-saving machinery was so extensively used; but now if men of flesh and blood cannot be found to take the strikers' places, Yankee

genius will invent some of steel that will do the
work as well:* Workmen are honorable, and
they would not, unless forced by necessity, desire to take the place of their fellow workers on
strike; but self-preservation and the wants of
wife and children appeal to them more strongly
than do the superficial ties of professional eti-
quette. The law will protect men in the enjoyment of their right to labor without interfer-
ence, wherever they choose to sell their services; and riot and failure only can follow from
this antiquated form of redress. The only hope
of the great mass of toilers lies in an increased
demand for labor. Can they increase the demand? They can.

Politicians of every party, statesmen of every
rank, and all who have eyes to see and ears to
hear, agree that prosperity primarily and principally consists in abundance of work at good
wages for all.

The preceding chapters have shown how the
introduction and use of labor-saving machinery

*The Secretary of the Federation of Employers
says: "Machinery is the answer of employers to
strikes."

has been displacing labor, year by year, at an alarming rate, and has been lessening the demand in every branch of manufacture and production. Labor-saving machinery has not benefited the workmen; it is no benefit to the country. It has wrought ruin to the small towns, and has driven the toilers to the great centers of population. Its use has benefited individual employers, but individual interest must yield to public good It has been fostered by legislation; by legislation it can be curtailed.

Organized labor can wield immense power, and the vast number of toilers guided by intelligence can determine the destiny of this land. They can make prosperity their hand-maiden, and she will come smiling at their call.

It would be a sad day for labor and for the country when organized labor should become a political party, in the sense conveyed by the word today; but the great common people can gain control of, or at least secure the balance of power in all the legislative bodies of the country. Representatives need not necessarily be from the ranks of labor, but they must be selected by labor and must, if possible, be in the employ of labor.

It is not merely a question of labor that confronts the land today, it is a question of prosperity, a question of the permanency of the government itself; and the patriotism of the country will rally to the aid of the standard bearers of justice and honor when called upon to rescue this free Republic from the clutch of death. The millions of toilers can vastly improve their own condition, and can confer immense benefits upon the country if they only awaken to the gravity of the situation and grasp the opportunity that lies within their reach.

Labor-saving machinery is the great rival of labor; and the first aim of labor's representatives should be to tax its employment and to curtail its use. They can begin with the prisons and penal institutions which are directly under the jurisdiction of the State, and abolish in these completely the use of all labor-saving machinery. The proper field for the employment of prison labor is in improving the highways; but if they must be employed in manufacture within prison walls, let them perform the work by hand. They will not make so much money for the politicians by this method; but they will also not do so much harm to honest labor. There is no need whatsoever for the use of labor-saving machinery within prison walls.

Representatives of labor on city and town councils could insist on the exclusion of labor-saving machinery on works which are under the immediate supervision of cities or towns, such as work on streets and parks. This method might cost a little more, but it would give work to a greater number of men, and it might be more economical in the end because it would be the means of keeping many a family off the books of the poor department.

These are perhaps matters of small moment, but they would aid perceptibly in increasing the demand for labor. It is useless to hope for reform in these matters from either of the great political parties, because all the faithful henchmen of either one will always place party policy above the public welfare.

If prosperity is ever again to gladden the homes and the hearts of the millions of toilers of this land it must come through the abolition of labor-saving machinery, or at least such a restriction in its use in manufacture and production that there may be employment for all. The country now produces more than it can consume, and prosperity cannot surely come by producing more, because they cannot find a market for their present products. Even those who believe that labor-saving machinery is the natural concomitant of enlightened nineteenth century civilization, admit* that it would require from fifty to one hundred million workers, by old methods, to produce the same amount that is now turned out by the present economic system; and yet hundreds of thousands of willing workers are now idle and cannot find employment.

It is idle folly to think that a change in the currency or in the tariff can bring permanent or even prolonged prosperity. The law of supply and demand governs production, and no change in the currency or the tariff can induce manu-

*Carroll D. Wright.

facturers and producers to turn out more products than they can find a market for, otherwise overproduction and consequent stagnation must necessarily follow.

Some Political Economists* claim that the whole progress of civilization consists in accomplishing greater or better results with the same or lesser effort. Labor-saving machinery according to this theory, should be the surest and about the only sign of progress in civilization; and as the United States leads the world in labor-saving inventions it must lead the van of civilized nations. The displacement of labor seems to be of no account in this calculation; the toilers must keep up with the procession or drop by the wayside and die.

Men are endowed with unalienable rights to life, liberty and the pursuit of happiness; and governments are instituted to secure these rights.** It is the duty of government, in order to preserve liberty, to protect every member of the society from the injustice or oppression of

* "Recent Economic Changes," Wells.
**Declaration of Independence.

every other member of it.*   It is also the duty
of government, as far as lies in its power, to
provide the means of happiness for all its subjects.   The economic theories of the present
day, which advocate the use of labor-saving machinery as a necessary element of progress and
civilization, and which seem to be accepted as
true by our statesmen and officials, are in direct
opposition to the above principles.   If millions
must suffer want and thousands starve that a few
hundred or a few thousand may prosper, then
government is failing in its purpose and this fin
de siecle civilization is lapsing into barbarism.
In what does our civilization differ from the civilization of ancient Rome or Greece?   They cultivated the fine arts.   Their sculpture, their
architecture, and their literature, are still the
models of the world.   Slavery existed then, and
the Roman had no regard for the rights or life
of any one who was not a citizen.

   The present generation witnessed the abolition of slavery here after a long civil war that
cost hundreds of thousands of lives, but there is

*Adam Smith.

a growing disposition to disregard the equality of rights in regard to the toilers.

Might, at least in fact, is right, and if the toilers wish to preserve their right to life, liberty and the pursuit of happiness, they must first attain power, then the world will give heed to their cause. The right to life includes the right to the means of preserving life, and the right to the pursuit of happiness includes the right to the means of procuring happiness, without any unjust curtailment of either one of these means by any economic conditions which enlarge the earnings of one class at the expense of any other. The use of labor-saving machinery has immensely curtailed the opportunities of employment and decreased the means of obtaining a livelihood.

Labor becomes less necessary every year in manufacture and production. Sixty per cent. of the earnings in production were paid in wages in 1850, and forty per cent. were the profits of capital. Now only seventeen per cent. of the earnings are paid in wages, and the balance, eighty-three per cent., is claimed by capital. The earnings of capital will continue to increase and the amount paid in wages will decrease in proportion as labor-saving machinery displaces hand work, until the workman will be nearly eliminated from manufacture and production. Only a mountebank could offer to remedy the evil by a change in the currency or the tariff.

The present economic method of manufacture has been favored by government and has been lauded by writers of political economy as the surest indication of progress. Every new invention designed to displace labor has been heralded through the land as another step in the march of progress. Where will it end? Work will be getting scarcer and scarcer as labor-saving machinery is introduced into new branches of industry, or greater improvement is made in the old inventions.

This is a comparatively new country; its resources are unrivaled; its opportunities should be unlimited. New countries offer a broader and richer field to enterprise in developing their resources, and give a greater amount of employment in proportion to their population than do those countries that have already attained wealth and a fixity in their commerce and progress.* Americans pride themselves on the strides their country is taking towards wealth and commercial supremacy, but its labor market is in a worse condition than is the labor in those European countries that came to a standstill centuries ago. This is a very abnormal condition, and is exceptional in the history of any fertile and progressive country in the world.

How can these conditions be changed, so that labor may be placed on a healthy basis and not only move forward with the progress of the country but also contribute its share of the necessary elements of prosperity? This can be done most effectively, and perhaps, only, by legislation.

If men can agree on the cause of this evil they can abolish or restrict it by legislation, but to do this men must be placed in legislative halls who cannot be swerved from their duty by the behests of any political boss or machine or by the gold of corporations or trusts. Do we need ex-

*Adam Smith.

traordinarily good men to come up to this standard? Not necessarily, but they must be elected
by labor, must be in the employ of labor, and
must agree to resign if labor requests them to
do so?*

Under present systems there is practically
no check upon legislators, and they are free to
vote away the rights of the people or to sell their
influence as their pleasure suggests or their
party leaders command, and they can rely upon
the power of machine politics to return them to
office, notwithstanding their record. The greatest crime in the eyes of party leaders is rebellion
against party policy. Party policy includes the
collection of vast sums for election purposes.
These millions come from trusts, corporations,
manufacturers and individuals, and must be re-
paid by legislation, which often is but the legislative transfer of public rights to private corporations.

This need not necessarily be the exclusive
work of labor; but labor is most directly inter-

* "The Workingmen's Political Labor Alliance"
was organized in Buffalo, April, 1897.

ested in this work, and on account of its numbers and organization it is in a position to put it in operation. The welfare of labor and the prosperity of the country depend upon a change in the methods of production. The wild schemes proposed by labor leaders, and the pitiful appeals for help are like the blind efforts of the drowning, clutching at straws to save them from death, and show the desperate condition to which they have been reduced. There is no prospect of more work for the multitudes in the future unless the methods of production are changed. The producing and manufacturing industries will even need fewer operatives as new labor-saving inventions are introduced or the old ones improved.

This country is now producing about one-third more than it can consume. A long line of fast vessels are carrying millions of bushels of our wheat to Europe. We are selling our steel tools and our steel rails in the English market, because we do not need men here in their manufacture. We are selling our carpets, our cloth, our cabinet ware and our boots and shoes all over

Europe, because we can manufacture cheaper than they can. The United States Government instructs its consuls to hunt up a market for our products in every country in the world. We cannot suppose that other countries will buy more of our products in the future than they do at present, because they too are as anxious to sell their goods and make money as are their Yankee friends. Our methods of manufacture will be imitated wherever the process of production can be cheapened, and our foreign trade is not likely to always show a large balance in our favor.

We must rely upon our home markets for healthful and permanent prosperity; and any system which tends to glut these markets without increasing the consuming powers of the land is false economy and the most baneful element in our trade. Diminishing the demand for labor lessens the consuming power of the great mass of toilers; because many are thrown out of work or their wages are lowered by sharp competition, and they must forego all luxuries and confine their purchases to the bare necessaries of life.

The extensive use of labor-saving machinery works two evils: it causes overproduction, and it occasions underconsumption. Overproduction is the universal cause of industrial depression; underconsumption is the logical effect of this cause. No nation can enjoy continued prosperity that is subject to either one of these evils; and when both exist at the same time, as they usually do, because one causes the other, then the depression becomes intense and like a contagious disease affects the financial life of many nations.

The United States cannot be freed from the evil of overproduction until the means of production are restricted. The means of production are vastly in excess of the powers of consumption; and whenever the markets suggest a demand or hold out a promise of fair profit, then all those means are hastily put in operation, and glut and stagnation must follow. There is no overproduction in certain lines of costly goods,*

---

* "Of special things, such as fine tools, there is never overproduction. They are too expensive to produce to be recklessly made to load up shelves." F. Gottfried.

in the manufacture of which labor-saving machinery has not been introduced to degrade
them, because men could not afford to allow the
capital invested to lie idle, and the supply never
exceeds the demand. The same principle would
control every branch of production if producers
had not been lured by greed into the use of labor-saving machinery to cheapen the cost of production and to increase the quantity of their
products. These greedy producers are like the
man who killed the goose that layed the golden
egg, they crippled the powers of consumption
by diminishing the demand for labor. Greed
is the formal cause of overproduction, and overproduction is the efficient cause of industrial depression.

Is the greed of a few individuals to be allowed to cause suffering to the whole nation?
How can this greed be checked? It can be
checked by legislation, either direct, or through
taxation. Laws can be passed to prohibit the use
of all merely labor-saving machinery, or these
may be taxed in such a manner as to practically
prevent their use.

This proposition may seem like a retrogression in civilization to some of our enlightened political economists; but the present system will soon lead to anarchy and revolution, and if our civilization requires the sacrifice of thousands of human beings to Mammon then the sooner this civilization is destroyed the better it will be for the human race.

It would not be wise to prohibit the use of all labor-saving machinery, as much of it is useful and even necessary for transacting the vast commerce of the world. In many branches of trade and production labor-saving machinery serves no other purpose except to substitute machine for hand work and to displace labor, for the sole purpose of lessening the cost of production. All such use of labor-saving inventions should be prohibited by law, or should be so heavily taxed that they could not compete with hand labor in a free market. If man has a right to life he has a right to the means of sustaining life; and it is the duty of government to prevent individuals from unnecessarily destroying or lessening these means which nature and a wholesome state of

society provide. These means arise from nature or from the natural conditions of society,
and no one has a right to wantonly destroy or
usurp them in such measure as to exclude others
from their enjoyment or to cause suffering from
want of them.

"The ultimate end of government is to secure
or provide for the greatest possible number, the
external conditions that make happiness possible."*   One of the principal aims of the Constitution of the United States is, "to promote
the general welfare,"** and the welfare of the
people may require the government to regulate
the methods of production. The government
regulates the commerce of the land, and it may
regulate the methods of production without in-
termeddling much more with private interests,
or of being guilty of paternalism. Laws regulating industry are not tyrannous in their pro-
hibitions, nor do they tend to paternalism in
their favors.***

* "Labor and the Popular Welfare." Mallock.
** Preamble to Constitution.
*** Nicholson.

The absolute prohibition of all labor-saving machinery in manufacture and production would place this country in a very disadvantageous position in regard to those adjacent countries that employ it, and these might flood our markets with their cheap products, and our toilers would be in a worse condition than at present. We can obviate this difficulty by an ample protective tariff. It would not be wise to abolish immediately all labor-saving machinery in every branch of industry; but three or four of the most extensive trades might be selected, in which the use of labor-saving machinery serves no other purpose than to cheapen the cost of production, and in these its use might be entirely prohibited or so restricted by taxation that it would amount to actual prohibition, and then the hand-made products of these industries might be protected from foreign competition by high protective tariff.

The branches of industry which offer the best field for this radical change are: cloth and clothing making; boot and shoe making, cigar and cigarette making, agriculture and carpentry

with its inimical adjunct—the planing mill.
These industries produce almost entirely for
home consumption, and they can only be in a
prosperous condition when the home markets
furnish a healthful demand for almost their entire products. When in full operation they
produce much more than can be consumed at
home, and cause stagnation and depression, yet
they do not give employment to one-fourth the
number of hands which should be required to
produce the same amount.

A change to hand work in these industries
would not injure any producer, because all would
be on the same footing, but it would immensely benefit labor, giving employment to
several times the number now engaged. Profits might be smaller, but the market would be
healthier; there would be a steady demand and
less competition, and the consuming power
would be greatly increased through the diffusion
of money among the consumers. The increased
demand for labor in those branches would re-
dound to the benefit of every other branch
of industry; because it would decrease the sup-

ply in general by offering inducements to men in other callings to enter these trades. Every one can see with half an eye that the present pitiable condition of labor is caused by a superabundant supply in excess of the demand, and this method would tend to produce an equilibrium, or even a slight balance in favor of labor. The country will never suffer from the excess of demand over supply of labor. Any such excess could easily be remedied, as it often has been in the past;* but it is passing strange that no effectual attempt has ever been made to honorably remedy the excess of supply. This can be remedied as well as can the excess of demand. It never has been, because legislators have never been convinced that it demanded attention. Parties interested in the welfare of labor were always either too insignificant to awaken public sympathy or too poor to interest our high-priced law makers in their cause.

Whatever opposition may be aroused against

*Wages were once regulated by law to prevent excessively high wages, labor was so scarce. Slaves were introduced into the Southern States on account of the scarcity of laborers.

the direct prohibition of labor-saving machinery in manufacture and production, it does not appear that any national objection can be offered against the taxation of the same.

Citizens are bound to support the government according to their ability, not only because they are able to contribute in proportion to their wealth, but also because the power and protection of the government are employed in the service of its citizens in protecting landed estates and commercial interests. The more wealth a man possesses the more power of the government is required, in various intricate ways, to preserve that wealth inviolable and secure its peaceful possession to its owner. The government promotes and protects the commerce and manufactures of the country. Our consuls in every land are instructed to report on the prospects of foreign markets for our products. Millions of dollars are spent every year by the government to promote navigation, to facilitate transportation, and to render distant markets accessible to the producer.

The manufacturers and producers are under special obligations to the government and should gracefully submit to increased taxation on account of the protection and assistance extended to them; their profits* have been increasing enormously in late years through the adoption of inventions protected by the government, though they have not been able to reap the full measure on account of overproduction. No laws are passed, no money is expended to improve the condition of the toiler, yet the greater portion of the taxes, under the present system, are drawn from his slender purse. The landlord, the grocer, the butcher, the merchant, pay their taxes from the profits they derive from rent, or from the sales of groceries, of meat or of clothing to the toiler and his family; and if their taxes are increased the landlord will raise the rent a little higher; the grocer will add a little more to the price of eggs, of butter, or of tea; the butcher will charge a

*Twenty-five years ago the share of profits in products of capital and labor were 60 and 40 per cent. respectively; now they are 87 and 17 per cent. respectively.

penny or two more for a pound of meat; the merchant will say the price of clothing has gone up and will charge a dollar more for a suit of clothes, and all of these will make the toilers pay the additional sum on their tax bills. Very few wealthy people pay the tax on personal property. A change, therefore, in the present system of levying taxes would seem to be a debt of justice which the State owes to labor.

"The power of production constitutes the only theoretically just basis of taxation. Men are bound to serve the State in the same degree in which they have the ability to serve themselves* The use of labor-saving machinery has enormously increased the power of production, and it should be made to bear its share of the burden of taxation. Its use gives men an enormous advantage over hand workers, and it constitutes a vast monopoly by practically excluding all hand labor from production. This will never be done on the theory that it is just and right; it will never be done until men are placed in our legislative halls whose inspirations

Walker. Ely.

will be a sense of duty, and who will legislate for the interests of the country and the rights of their fellow men.

Let labor concentrate all its energies on the work of placing such men in power, on the distinct platform of the direct prohibition or heavy taxation of the use of all mere labor-saving machinery* in production, and there will be no more call for their perennial fatuous strikes and their vain appeal for public sympathy. They can do incalculable good to their cause and their country. It remains for the toilers to initiate this great work, because they are most directly interested in its success, but millions of patriotic hearts will respond to the call and will second their efforts. The great political parties of the present day are too irretrievably mersed in the spoils-hunting policy, or too trust-ridden to ever start such an unremunerative movement as the redemption of this country from its industrial thraldom.

"The Congress shall have power to levy and collect taxes . . . and provide . . . for the

*Such as merely displaces labor.

general welfare."* It is clearly within the province of Congress to levy a tax on labor-saving machinery; and the general welfare will not only justify Congress in imposing this tax, but does most earnestly demand it from Congress as a measure of public necessity. In what other way can work be given to the thousands and the hundreds of thousands of idle men? Government may not be obliged to provide employment for idle men; but it should protect its weaker citizens from the rapacity of the strong, and it must prevent its citizens from restricting, destroying, or monopolizing the means of earning a livelihood in such a manner that others must suffer from want of them.

The House of Representatives is the proper place to inaugurate this law. Labor may not be able to secure a majority of the House, but they could secure at least enough members to make their influence felt and to hold the balance of power. Public opinion would come to their aid if the question was fairly placed before the country.

*Article 1, Sec. 8, Constitution of the United States.

The great bonanza farms of the West and Southwest, that are forcing the real farmers into poverty should be abolished by law. They are vast speculative monopolies, entirely opposed to the interests of agriculture and the prosperity of the land. The general prosperity of the land depends in great measure upon the prosperity of the farming population. The condition of the farming population has been growing worse from year to year. The young people have been abandoning farming, simply because there is no money in it. Our real farmers cannot compete with the great bonanza farms of the West and South. Labor-saving machinery have made the bonanza farms possible. Abolish labor-saving agricultural machines, or restrict their use, and the bonanza monsters will disappear. Thousands will again take to farming life, which afforded honorable and profitable living before and will do so again when restored to its former condition. Every form of industry will profit by the renewed life of agriculture.

There is ample field for the genius, the numbers and the power that labor can send forth to

bring real prosperity back to the land—a prosperity that is not merely measured by the clear-
ings of the banks or the volume of trade; but a
prosperity which includes work and good wages
for the laborer, the mechanic, the clerk, the
tradesman of every branch of industry, and comfort and happiness in their homes. Those people who are most interested, the vast body of
toilers, are numerous enough to sweep everything before them, if they are only wisely
guided, and secure able men to direct their
councils and to control their acts.

There is no hope for the improvement of the
labor market by strikes or unions so long as there
are thousands of idle men ready and willing to
accept any employment that will bring them
enough money to ward off starvation; yet the
country is not over-crowded, its resources are
not exhausted. There is territory enough in the
United States to accommodate a population of
five hundred million.* The resources of the
land are almost unlimited, but they have been

*Germany and England have a population about
equal to that of the United States, yet their combined territory is no larger than the State of Texas.

badly managed—they have been monopolized by a few who in their greed have lost sight of the rights of their fellow men. Law alone can restore the country to healthful and prosperous conditions, and the power to establish this law lies in the hands of the toilers.

Toilers have only themselves to blame if they do not make industrial methods conform to the true requisites of prosperity and to the measure of their wants. They may plead in vain to our law makers for justice, and they will not be heard except their good will and their votes are wanted, and these may be secured by some trifling law of doubtful value. But why should they appeal to others for justice when they have the power in their own hands of meting out justice to themselves? Men may clamor against a change which they believe to be a retrogression in progress and civilization; but once the new laws are in operation they will cheerfully obey, and will learn to bless the wisdom that has forced prosperity on the land.

The wage-earners form fully three-fourths* of

*Eugene Debs.

the population of the country. Majority rules in this land; and if the wage-earners understand their wants and the changes necessary in industrial conditions to give work to the unemployed, they will have only themselves to blame if they do not obtain all they desire. Intelligence is the first essential of success. When the toilers have full knowledge of the evil of the present system of production, and a complete understanding of the changes necessary to abolish the evil, and unite in laboring for the proposed end, no power can restrain them from accomplishing their purpose.*

Labor in general is worthy of as much attention from this government as any other department of State, and it should have a representative from its own ranks, or, at least, one well versed in its wants, in a Cabinet position. Agriculture is represented in the Cabinet, though the

*Intelligent, united and concerted action by his ballot, and through this to control the law-making bodies of the United States, is the working-man's only hope. "The workman makes as much use of his ballot as a howling savage would make of a chronometer. He can by voting work out his own salvation. When will we begin?" New York Evening Journal.

duties of this department seem to be limited to distributing seed among the farmers. The condition of the farming population has been continually growing worse, because no intelligent effort has been made to advance their interests. If the Department of Agriculture had advised the President, years ago, to urge Congress to abolish the bonanza farms of the West, or to limit by law the number of acres any one party could possess, or to put a practically prohibitory tax upon labor-saving agricultural machinery, farming would be in a prosperous condition to-day; and every branch of industry would have been benefited by the impetus given to agriculture.

The establishment of the Labor Bureau was a graceful recognition of the rights of labor to government attention. The Bureau should be in thorough sympathy with the aims of labor; it should advocate labor's cause; and it should urge the passage of laws that would improve the condition of the wage-earners. The Bureau seems now to be taken up considerably with useless juggling of the inconsequent figures of the census, trying to prove by statistics that the toilers receive better wages and have more work than at any time in the past half century. There is a suspicion also that the octopus arms of trusts and monopolies have enveloped the Bureau in their folds.*

The Patent Office is a prime factor in the birth and growth of trusts. Exclusive rights are given to parties to use some process in production, and it is an easy matter then to drive hand labor from the field, with the assistance of government. Patents should not be given to inventions, which are nothing more than cunning devices for robbing men of the means of earning a livelihood. Why not issue a patent to the expert cracksman to secure to him the exclusive right of opening safes, or to the shrewd burglar, who has some secret of opening doors and windows? These are only slightly more direct forms of spoilation than those which have the

*At a recent convention of mayors of cities and other interested parties held in one of our Western cities to discuss municipal ownership of franchises, street railways, gas, etc., the Labor Bureau was represented by a high official who favored monopolies and corporations.

sanction of government through the Patent Office.

Some criterion of worth should be required in every invention before a patent is issued for its use. Inventions which have no other object than to displace labor employed at good wages should not be tolerated; they should be condemned by the Labor Bureau as inimical to the interests of the class of citizens this Bureau is supposed to represent. Inventions which lighten the burdens of toil without displacing employed labor are a blessing; but those which merely displace labor only serve to gratify the greed of some, whilst they add to the sum of human misery in the world. Every invention which is intended for the field of labor should have the approval of the Labor Bureau before a patent is issued for it, and before it is allowed in use

Organized labor* looks now to shorter hours for a solution of the problem of the unemployed and higher wages. Shorter hours of labor would certainly give employment to a greater number; but this change would not improve the condition

*Samuel Gompers, N. Y. Herald, Jan. 2, 1898.

of labor unless they can obtain the same wages. Success in any labor movement depends upon the condition of the labor market. If the demand for labor exceeds the supply labor can stipulate its own terms as to wages and the hours; but if the supply vastly exceeds the demand, then labor will be willing to accept any terms. The government will sustain the right to private contract, and prospective starvation has made many a brave army capitulate.

The eight-hour day would only bring temporary relief, even if it could be universally enforced, which is not at all probable. The displacement of labor by machinery would continue just the same, and the cause of the evil would be as vigorous as ever. Remove the cause and the disease will be entirely eradicated. A few employers may reduce the working hours, but there will also be a proportionate cut in wages, unless conditions are changed. Employers may do as they please now, because the labor supply is vastly in excess of the demand. Employees may strike; but their places will be taken by others, or machines will be substituted for men. When the demand for labor equals, or exceeds the supply, then the toilers can make their own terms and the employers will be forced to meet them.

Remedies for the industrial depression, which has settled over the land, were proposed in the politics of the two great parties at the last Presidential election; but neither one was founded upon the true cause of the evil, and, consequently, could not bring permanent relief. Statesmen and politicians advocated these remedies as popular means of gaining public favor rather than from profound study of the causes of the evil. Protection for our industries can bring very little relief whilst our own cheap methods of production enable us to undersell Europeans in their own markets; and greater quantity of money cannot cure the ill whilst millions are lying idle awaiting profitable investment.

Give plenty of work at good wages and the "hard times" will vanish, never more to return as long as the wages and work will last; and these can be made permanent by the reforms indicated in our methods of production.

CHAPTER XI.
THE OUTLOOK.

Much suffering will, no doubt, always exist in the world. The volume of business is so vast and complicated that stagnations and failures in some branches must necessarily come. Men will be improvident, and will fail to profit by the opportunities which nature and commercial conditions hold out to them. Production is vastly in excess of consumption in all the manufacturing and civilized countries of the world. The science of production has reached a high degree of perfection and is still capable of almost unlimited further development, whilst the science of distribution* is yet in its rude embryonic state, and is deteriorating instead of progressing. The earth is capable of producing food enough to supply many times the number of its present inhabitants, and the rates of transportation are so cheap and the methods so rapid that no portion of the world need necessarily suffer from want of the necessaries of life.

*By distribution is meant the distribution of the income derived from products.

With such abundance of products and facilities for sending goods to every part of the world, the only drawback to general prosperity and happiness would be inability to purchase. This feature of the social and industrial problem has never seemed to merit the attention of our political economists and statesmen, although it is necessarily connected with prosperity. Where there is underconsumption, there will be overproduction, unless there be a famine; yet our manufacturers, economists and statesmen act on the principle that prosperity depends upon production alone, and they cripple the consuming power in the attempt to increase the powers of production. This is about as foolish as for a man to expect to run faster by shackling one leg in order to concentrate all his power on the other; both are necessary for rapid progress. There is money in producing; there is none in consuming. This may be the secret of the difference of interest taken in these two subjects by our public men.

Prosperity will never find a permanent abode in this land as long as the consuming powers of

the nation are in a crippled condition; and the
consuming powers will ever remain crippled until a check is placed upon the use of labor-saving
machinery.   The volume of business and trade
for the past few months* has been enormous,
and has surpassed, most probably, anything in
the history of the country; yet there are thousands of men out of employment.   This extraordinary volume of trade is caused by the failure
of grain crops in India and South America,
(which supply about one-half the wheat to European markets), and by the ability of American
manufacturers to produce certain lines of
goods** cheaper than they can be produced in
Europe.   These two causes of extraordinary demand for American products are accidental and
transitory, and cannot be relied upon as a permanent source of prosperity.   We are very seldom
called upon to furnish more than a certain ratio
of the European food supply, and our ability to
undersell European manufacturers offers no
hope of future stability.

*October, 1898.
**Steel rails, tools, carpets, and machines of vari-
ous kinds.

Russia, India, South America and the United States make up the shortage of the wheat supply for Great Britain and Continental Europe. The wheat crops of India and of some of the South American States were partial failures this year, and this created an extraordinary demand for the food and grain supply of the United States. The price of wheat more than doubled (in value), and this accidental demand started the wheels in every branch of industry, and inspired people with the confidence of prosperity returned.

Our bonanza farms, with their labor-saving harvesters, reapers, and threshers, can put wheat on the market cheaper than any other country in the world. Russia and South America are adopting our methods and our machines, and, with the aid of India and cheap labor, may yet be able to force United States wheat from the European markets. The present extraordinary foreign demand is accidental and fictitious, and it would be folly to base upon this our hope of continued prosperity.

We are selling our manufactured goods in every part of the world where we can find a market for them, and the markets at present are extensive and favorable. We can undersell European manufacturers even in their own markets, though labor is considered cheaper there, because our labor-saving machinery displaces skilled labor and increases the output and lessens the cost of production. Yankee agents are first in every field, and like swarms of summer insects, they swoop down upon every promising field to gather in the substance and the wealth that it yields. The zenith of civilization, according to the views of our up-to-date business men, would be to induce the savage to dress in our sweat-shop, machine-made clothing, and to cover his feet with our factory-made shoes. Virtue, morality, enlightenment, the fine arts, are antiquated ideas, good enough for the ladies or retired merchants. Education is good, but only in as much as it fits one for a successful financial career. Business, trade and wealth are the standards of civilization today.

Can the United States maintain her supremacy in foreign markets? Labor-saving machinery enables our manufacturers to produce at less cost, and to undersell their foreign competitors;* but will not these foreign manufacturers adopt labor-saving machinery, and, with their cheaper labor, drive American goods out of their markets? It would be presumption to assume that there is not scientific knowledge or inventive genius enough in Europe to construct machines which will cheapen the cost of production by displacing labor.

England once had a monopoly of labor-saving machines used in the textile industries, and only necessity, "the mother of inventions," led American genius to surpass them in this field. Necessity may arouse European manufacturers to employ inventive genius that will construct machines which will enable them to successfully compete with their American rivals; and then, where will our manufacturers find markets for their enormous yields of cheap products?

Permanent prosperity can only come from the

*The London Times says: "American machine tools by the hundreds of thousands of dollars worth are sent, freight paid, for thousands of mills across the ocean to England, France, Russia, Japan and China. (See preceding note.)

constant and ample demand of home markets;* and this constant demand can only be maintained when the actual consumption about equals the powers of production.** Methods of production that cripple consumption are evils that should be remedied by legislation, because they violate the rights of individuals and they are inimical to the general interests of the country.

The United States leads the world today in the use of labor-saving machinery in the various branches of manufacture and production, and the United States is more subject than any other country in the world to the fluctuations of fitful progress and long continued industrial depression. Other nations may be subject to these changes, but only in proportion to their use of labor-saving machinery. Speculation or crop failure may cause temporary embarrassments in

*Chauncey Depew, interview on the cause of " hard times."

**This does not mean that their output should be limited to the demands of home consumption, but that the methods used for supplying the home market should be such as would give abundant employ ment to all forms of labor.

any land, which may be easily overcome; but depressions arising from industrial methods cannot be remedied except by a change or removal of the cause.

France, Germany, Italy, Spain, Austria and the minor countries of Europe scarcely ever suffer from long continued periods of "hard times;" yet they are able to support enormous standing armies, and their people are fairly prosperous. The man may not get very high wages, but there is work of some kind for everybody. The cause of their continued prosperity is simple enough; they do not use labor-saving machinery which would flood their markets with cheap products, would cripple their consuming power, and would deprive their men of employment. Their cities show every evidence of wealth, health, comfort, convenience and splendor that can be found in what we are pleased to consider our own more progressive land. They excel us in literature, architecture, painting, sculpture and music. Their civilization is refined; ours is machine made.

European merchants and manufacturers will soon learn that there is money in our methods, and they may make use of labor-saving inventions to drive our products out of their markets. Let us hope, not only on account of our own interests, but more especially on account of the general welfare of the congested populations of Europe, that our patent labor-saving devices will never be introduced in their industries. This country is better able than any European country to stand the enormous displacement of labor caused by the use of labor-saving inventions. We have boundless territory and unlimited resources; but even these are not sufficient to offset the evils of our industrial methods. No European country could stand the enormous displacement of labor that has taken place here without frightful ruin and extensive want.

What benefits have these labor-saving machine methods conferred upon this country? A few individuals have made fortunes out of them, whilst the country has been forced to the verge of bankruptcy in its private affairs and its public relations. The Government was forced to secure a loan to meet its expenses. Banks would not make loans because they could not make collections. Manufactories were idle because there was no market. Millions of men were forced out because machines had taken their places, and had flooded the markets with goods for which there was no demand. All this time France,* as well as the other Continental European nations, enjoyed uninterrupted industrial prosperity because they had not introduced the abnormal factor of labor-saving machinery into their industries, to destroy the equilibrium between consumption and production, and to bring the spectre of "hard times" into their lands by depriving the toilers of their employment.

Whilst millions in the United States are walking the streets looking for employment, some men offering to sell themselves as slaves** that they may obtain food and shelter, little Japan, a nation we look upon as semi-barbarous, is seen calling her sons from Hawaii and other

*Testimony of editor Cleveland Leader.

**Two cases were recently advertised in the New York World. They were young, healthy, well educated men who offered to sell themselves as slaves.

lands to work at home, so abundant is the
employment and so prosperous the condition of
the country.* Wages are high; yet they cannot
compare with the United States in export trade
or internal resources; but they have no labor-
saving devices to destroy their prosperity. Nearly
all their products are made by hand,** and this
secures steady employment and good wages to
their toilers, and permanent prosperity to their
land. They are fast advancing toward commercial and political supremacy in the East, and some
think they are arriving at naval supremacy on
the Pacific Ocean.

It is short-sighted policy to allow the greed
of a few individuals to retard the progress of
the whole nation. Those semi-barbarous Ori-
entals may yet teach us that true progress consists in the welfare of the whole people, and not
in the enormous wealth of a few who have been
favored by laws and special privileges.

Many sensible and prominent men are inclined
to look with favor upon a modified form of com-

*Nargaski correspondent New York Sun.
**About the only labor-saving machinery in use
there is two American saw mills.

munism, "municipal socialism," as a remedy for the ills which are afflicting political and urban life. They see that trusts and monopolies are able to buy up legislative bodies and throurh them secure valuable privileges and franchises without just cempensation to the people, and they are lured into believing that it would be better for the people, through the municipality, to retain the ownership of these public franchises. This would only transfer the control from corporate bodies to political rings, and from comparatively harmless sources of individual wealth, they would become powerful engines of political corruption. Better, in this case: "to bear those ills we have, than fly to others we know not of."

Private ownership of institutions that serve the public is more in accordance with the liberty of our land than municipal absorption * of individual enterprise, and private corporations will

*The experience of Brazil with her railways under state control should be a warning against municipal ownership of works that employ great bodies of men. The railway which should pay well was run at a loss, and twice the number of men necessary were given employment because they were friends of those in office.

render better service than political parties.   If
private corporations can be made to pay for the
use of privileges in proportion to their value,
there will be no need to have recourse to frater-
nalism or socialism to remove the evil in many
private monopolies.   These monopolies are only
evil because they are not obliged to pay for the
use of public property, or because they evade
the just taxation for government protection
which renders their business so enormously
lucrative.

European nations are already awakening to
a realization of the injury to their commercial
and industrial interests by allowing their
markets to be flooded by the cheap products of
American labor-saving machinery.   Trades
unions of Scotland have declared against the
importation of cheap American ready-machine-
made joinery.   Poor as, we think, their carpenters and joiners are paid, they are not so
degraded as our machine-made goods would
make them.   Count Goluchowski,* the Austro-

*Address to Austrian and Hungarian delega-
tions, Nov. 21, 1897.

Hungarian Minister of Foreign Affairs, appeals to all the nations of Europe to unite in a vigorous defense of their home industries against the "crushing competition of Trans-Atlantic nations." "We must fight," he says, "shoulder to shoulder against the common danger, to protect the vital interests of the people of Europe." As each of the immediate preceding centuries has presented some particular grave universal problem for solution, the approaching twentieth century will be noted for the great industrial and commercial struggle. The advance guard of American machine-made products is already invading European markets, and the succeeding hosts of the main army threaten, unless checked, to conquer the commerce of the world, and to destroy the industrial life of all Europe.*

If our products be excluded from European markets, where can we find a market for our enormous surplus stock? Several departments

*Ibid. Speech before Chamber of Commerce of Creydon, Nov. 23, 1897.

Herr Hammacher, in the German Reichstag, repeats the note of warning uttered by Count Golu-

of the government are enlisted in the service of the manufacturers, and are instructed to find foreign markets for their goods. Merchants are seeking markets in South America, because we can undersell their cheap labor products.* The Rt. Hon. Charles Ritchie, president of the London Board of Trade, also warns British manufacturers against American competition. "Americans," he says, "are ousting the British from their own markets, because freedom in the use of labor-saving machinery enables Americans to manufacture at less cost."

Our industries can only be in a healthful and prosperous condition when the means of producing to supply the home consumption will give employment to nearly all our workers. If production were now limited to supply the

chowski in Austria, and adds that it behooves Germany to be ready for the industrial struggle against America in the next century.

*They now propose to appoint military attaches to each of the South American legations, whose sole office will be to find markets for military stores of American manufacture.

Men propose to fit out a large vessel with our machine-made goods, and to exhibit them in all the South American countries, in the hope of extensively enlarging our markets by the cheapness of our products.

home demand, ruin and general depression would follow; because our system is built on the false notion that production alone is prosperity.

We are the greatest producing country today in the world. Our resources are unlimited. Our fertile fields can furnish food for many times the number of our people. Our manufacturing facilities are vastly in excess of home consumption. Unless we can keep consumption up to the rapid progress of production stagnation must follow. This is all the more certain as present methods of production do not even now give employment to all our workers. Some check must be put upon our outrageous methods of producing if we ever hope to see permanent prosperity in our land.

One of the great evils of the present, and one which threatens to increase instead of diminish as the years roll by, is the existence of trusts that monopolize certain lines of trade and force small dealers out of business. Trusts invade every branch of trade and manufacture. Attempts have been made to legislate against them, but party interests are too closely allied with the prosperity of the trusts to foster any real opposition to them in our legislatures, and wily politicians succeed in inserting some annulling clause in anti-trust laws to hoodwink the people.

Machinery methods of production, and the factory system, have favored the existence of trusts. With all the manufactures, in certain lines, confined to a few large establishments, it is an easy matter to bring production under one control. Greater capital is required to manufacture by machinery than by hand, and this, of itself, tends towards the concentration of production. Division of labor, which is a necessary concomitant of machinemanufacture,* requires production on a large scale, and this also favors monopoly.

Hand methods cannot compete with machine production. Hand make, in nearly every branch of production, is superior in workmanship, finish and value to the machine-made goods; yet

---

*This word is now something of a misnomer when applied to machinery. Originally it meant the making by hand. Hands have very little to do in modern methods of manufacture.

the former cannot compete with the latter on account of the vast disparity in the cost of production. Independent hand producers were obliged to abandon their little shops and unite with the great modern manufactories, or drop out of the business; and then it was but another step, and quite a natural one too, to unite the manufactories under one head, and thus form a trust.

All trusts may not have been built up in this manner, but modern systems of manufacture favor their formation. Then trusts are growing in number, and threaten to engross every production, every business. Laws seem ineffectual in arresting their progress, because they have become more powerful than law. They direct the making of laws; and they influence their interpretation and escape their penalty.

It seems reasonable to believe that the most effectual means to abolish trusts would be to remove the conditions which have made them possible. Many of these trusts could not exist under the old system of hand work. Every little town and hamlet then had some little manufactory or shop in which raw material was made into articles of use or luxury for the inhabitants of the town and surrounding country. It would be practically impossible to unite these innumerable little shops under one control, or to form a trust out of these thousands of independent producers.

Some of our wise men proclaimed that confidence was the only thing necessary to restore prosperity; and when confidence came after a protracted period of limited production, on account of glutted markets, producers set all their machinery agoing, and turned out goods at an enormous rate. The tariff, which favored home industries, and the temporary settlement of the money question, both helped to restore the long lost confidence; but the sluggish markets, the lowered wages, the shortened employment, the many idle, but willing, hands are beginning to convince our wise men that something more than confidence is necessary for permanent prosperity.

The means of production are being constantly increased, notwithstanding the fact that present facilities are vastly in excess of the demand. Every day new methods are devised for increasing the producing power and lessening the cost; and most of these methods are established on the principle of displacing hand work by machinery, as this seems to be the most effective means of accomplishing the desired result. The Patent Office* is overwhelmed with devices for displacing labor, and yet our statesmen are planning all sorts of schemes, but the true one, to bring back prosperity.

Producers must look to the great mass of toilers for consumption, and it would be wise policy to offer every facility for increasing the consuming power in order to increase the sales. Greed, however, seems to have more influence over the acts of men than wisdom; and our producers cripple the consuming power and increase their productions in the expectations of greater gain. Foreign demand for our products must increase at an enormous rate to keep pace with our enormously increased production. Where

---

*There were twenty-five thousand new patents presented to the Patent Office last year.

can we find this market ?   Europe is already
combining against our cheap machine-made
goods.   The mechanics of other lands are pro-
testing against the use of our machine-made
goods in their countries, because they are not
able to compete with them, and the~ degrade
their trades and lower wages.

Americans boast of their ingenuity which
enables their producers to sell their goods at a
profit in countries where labor is very cheap.
But what benefit is there in the system ?   Do
the workers of America profit by this system ?
There is not work* enough here for all the toilers,
even under the present enormous productions;
and wages are only kept up to the living point
by the continual and persistent struggle of
trades unions.   Does the government profit by
the enormous export trade?   The government
has hard work to keep from bankruptcy ; it

---

*"Men in this nineteenth century are today with-
out any other alternative than to steal or starve.   I
meet them every day.   They are good men of the city,
but they are unfortunate. They are not to blame."
Mayor Jones, Toledo.

is continually running behind its actual expenditures.*

A few shrewd producers, operators and brokers make enormous fortunes out of the machine-producing systems whilst the great mass of toilers and the country in general, are in far poorer condition than they would be under the old method of hand work and slow production. If all this is true now, with an enormous export trade, general depression must soon follow when our foreign trade is notably lessened in volume.

The shortage in the wheat supply of Europe has created an abnormal demand for our grain, and has given an impetus to all our industries by placing money in the hands of the farmers; but this demand is only temporary and may not exist again for many years. Even with the present enormous exports,** our producing capacity

---

*The governments of Europe can support enormous armies and still have a balance in their treasuries, whilst ours with an insignificant budget runs behind.

**The exports this year (1897) have excelled the billion dollar mark, the highest in our history.

is not fully employed,* and thousands of idle but willing men are walking the streets looking for work; yet all our clairvoyant wise men can see Prosperity's rays advancing over the mountain tops, dispelling the gloom that has long settled over the land. It may be only an ignis fatuus that these wise men see, for present conditions do not indicate proximate permanent prosperity. We are now producing for foreign markets, yet not over one-half or three-fourths of our producing capacity is in actual operation, and it seems as if this amount must decrease instead of increase, because the abnormal demand for products was caused by the accidental shortage in the food supply of the European markets.

Europe is discussing means and methods of supplying its own markets with food products and manufactured goods to the exclusion of the American article. We have displaced a larger amount of high priced labor with machinery,

*Carroll D. Wright says only about 75 per cent. of our capacity to produce is now employed. (Note to N. Y. World, Dec. 12, 1897.) Very probably much less than 75 per cent. in actual operation, and the proportion may be nearer 45 per cent. than 75 per cent.—T. D.

and have lessened the cost of production; but they may go farther in the economic process than we have, and may thus force our goods out of their markets.

Labor leaders resort to all plausible expedients to improve the condition of the toilers, but they do not seem to make much progress; they are even losing ground. We cannot hope that men will meekly submit to conditions which deprive them of their constitutional right to the means of pursuing happiness, and if they find that the peaceful methods of reason and agitation fail, it would not be surprising to see them resort to force. We depend in great measure now upon foreign markets for the sale of our surplus products. If our foreign trade should diminish, our industries must suffer. All European nations seem more intent now upon extending trade than upon acquiring territory; and it is their policy to exclude American products not only from their own markets, but also from the East. Loss of our foreign markets would cripple our commerce, and would inflict incalculable loss upon our home prosperity. Our statesmen see, in the prospective dismemberment of China, a menace to our commerce in the East. European control in China would not only exclude our products from that country, but would introduce a new industrial competitor into the world that would deprive America of her commercial supremacy. "We cannot permit this without sinking to the position of a third or fourth rate nation, helpless, degraded, without influence among the nations of the earth."*

If ever such dire foreboding should come true, we may assign not the dismemberment of China, nor the loss of foreign markets, but our own stupid ideas of industrial progress as the cause of the disaster. Why should our national supremacy depend upon China, or upon any other foreign country? We have all the elements of stable greatness in our own land; why, then, should we depend upon other countries for our prosperity? It is an element of decay in our national life when we must depend upon foreign nations for our internal prosperity and strength.

*Senator Fuller in the New York World, Jan. 3, 1898. He feared that Russia and Germany would monopolize the trade of the East and drive our commerce from that part of the world.

The low rumblings of discontent are heard here and there over the earth like the crunching of stones in a volcano in the throes of an eruption. These are the protests of labor against the industrial slavery into which they are being led. It is a warning which Nature always gives of impending disaster. The remedy for all our ills lies in the hands of the people. The people make the laws; the people are the government. But the people only bellow and destroy when their rights are trampled on and they are injured, like the huge elephant that uses his immense physical power to smash everything about as evidence of his rage.

This land of freedom and joyful liberty should not be the home of discontent; should not be favorable to the growth of wild anarchy or the spirit of communism. These are associated in our minds with lands where liberty is unknown, where the knout of the master silences the protest of the serf, and where the will of the ruler is law. The tyrant's domain is anarchy's home. Anarchy is rebellion against law, but where the people make the laws it should not thrive. Com-

munism should not live in a land of vast opportunities that are open to all, and where success
is the reward of individual energy, talent and
worth. These wild exotics, anarchy and communism, have found this land congenial to their
spirits and the laws favorable to their life.

Men are not satisfied with the opportunities of
attaining wealth which bounteous nature and the
conditions of a civilized society offer; but they
prey upon their fellow men, and make them
serve as the instruments of their greed. Men
suborn legislatures, and secure laws which enrich
them at the expense of their fellow men. No
tyrant's rule is more obnoxious than the servitude
engendered by unjust laws. What matters it to
the subjects whether an unjust law is born of the
over-weening pride of the heartless tyrant, or the
insidious bribe of the greedy monopolist ? The
slavery is the same. There is even greater usurpation of rights in the latter case. Men more will-
ingly resign to power than to fraud; and anarchy
may as readily be engendered in the home of the
free as in the land of the tyrant.

We fondly believe that our land is free from the ills of a despot's rule. We elect our rulers; we make our laws. The downtrodden of other lands fly hither for protection, and for the enjoyment of liberty denied in their native homes. The outlaws have come too, not to enjoy liberty, but to teach their fellow men to rebel against the tyranny of free institutions. Anarchy and its kindred monster, communism, have found some favor in this land.* Communism, in a modified form, is advocated by men of different callings as a remedy for the evils of municipal and state government. Men can learn to hate the work of their own hands. Institutions that have grown up under the fostering care of our laws have become distasteful, and men are crying out against their existence.

The red flag of anarchy would find no favor here if men were not dissatisfied with their lot. Foreign followers of this mad delusion should be charmed and converted from their wild dreams, when they reach these shores, by the advantages

*Prince Propotkin claims that they are rapidly advancing here, whilst others maintain that all the followers of these principles are foreigners.

of free government and the opportunities of individual liberty. Instead of being lured to America to enjoy the blessings of liberty, they have come here to propogate their theories. Free government must fail when anarchy can find friends in a free land. They are not led hither by love, but by hate and hope. Like the vultures that scent the carrion from afar, they imagine that the dissolution of our national existence is near, and they are lured hither by the hope of prey.

New economic methods are driving the British workmen to the wall. Labor-saving machinery is rapidly displacing hand work, so that the British manufacturer may compete with his American rival. British trades unions have just abandoned the greatest struggle in their history for better conditions. They contended for a shorter day, for eight hours, in the hope that this would create a greater demand for labor; but they lost; they cannot successfully cope with machinery in economic production. When peaceable methods of resistance to injustice come to naught, the next step will be to resort to force.

When the proletariat believe that force is necessary to repel the invaders of their rights and to protect their lives, then reason flies, and all the destructive instincts of the wild and maddened animal come into play. Rank, wealth, property and power must give way before this ungovernable force.*

Let the cry of revolution be heard in England and it will soon be repeated in New York. Americans are patient and patriotic. They love their country, their institutions, their liberty and homes. It is this very love which would lead Americans to rebel against the usurpation of their rights and the destruction of their homes. Men may be driven to desperation by free bodies as well as by tyrannical despots. Americans freed the black slaves by force of arms, and the carnage of war may be necessary to free the white toilers from industrial slavery.

No one would like to see this fair land devastated by the horrors of war; to see the young and

*The oldest and wisest statesman of England, Gladstone, believes that the greatest danger that threatens England at the present time is not the military power of any of the European nations, but the trades unions of dissatisfied British workmen.

the middle-aged severing the tender ties of home, never more to return; yet such is the greed and obstinacy of men that, where important interests are involved, they will resort to arms rather than be guided by reason.

This should be a land of happy homes, of plenty and content. Its resources are practically limitless and inexhaustible. There is abundance for all; but some choose to despoil their fellow men instead of obtaining their share from the great storehouse of Nature, or through the honorable methods of professional, business or industrial life. Plenty or Want will reign over the land at the call of men. Nature has boundless stores of wealth; and the opportunities of advancement are without limit in this free land. What shall our future be ? Shall it be a future of prosperity, of progress, of peace and content; or shall it be a future of ruin, of want, of desolation and decay ? It will be whatever we decide to make it.

www.ingramcontent.com/pod-product-compliance
Lightning Source LLC
Chambersburg PA
CBHW030814020726
47499CB00006B/1911